Love in Every Stitch

Love in Every Stitch

Stories of Knitting and Healing

Lee Gant

VIVA
EDITIONS

Published in the United States by Viva Editions, an imprint of Start Midnight, LLC, 375 Hudson Street, Twelfth Floor, New York, New York 10014.

Printed in the United States.
Cover design: Scott Idleman/Blink Design
Cover photograph: C Squared Studios/Getty Images
Text design: Frank Wiedemann
First Edition.
10 9 8 7 6 5 4 3 2 1

Trade paper ISBN: 978-1-63228-018-3
E-book ISBN: 978-1-63228-029-9

Library of Congress Cataloging-in-Publication Data

Gant, Lee.
  Love in every stitch : stories of knitting and healing / Lee Gant.
     pages cm
   ISBN 978-1-63228-018-3 (paperback)
  1. Knitting--Therapeutic use. 2. Knitting--Psychological aspects.
I. Title.
  RM735.7.K54G36 2015
  746.43'2--dc23
                              2015002768

table of contents

I SPENT MANY TROUBLED years standing in front of the mirror with my face pressed close to the glass, peering into each pupil, trying to see all the way into myself. But there was always something blocking my view, like a piece of paper, something dark. I wanted to believe that there was a good person living inside of me, but I didn't know how to connect to her.

For years I betrayed myself, acting out and doing bad things. It took a great deal for me to believe that I belonged somewhere in this world, that I was worthy, and that my behaviors could be forgiven. My only choices became death or jail or change. Eventually, alcohol and drugs brought me to my knees, and it was then that knitting saved my life.

Knitting gave me a choice to do something different. I found direction and purpose and the capacity to share. I found accomplishment, self-worth, and success.

I still have anxieties, but when I look in the mirror today, the block is gone. There are times when I falter, but when I do, I know how to get back on track. I knit.

To those of you who already knit and crochet, I hope you'll teach someone else, because you never know whose life you might save.

To those of you who don't, I hope some of these

stories of hope, sharing, and second chances will inspire you to learn.

All you have to do is ask.

Sunshine Is a Color

THE BRIGHTNESS OF THE sun scrunches my face, and rainbow-colored sparklers spin behind my eyes. A jackhammer pounds its rat-tat-tat into the back of my head. Hungover and nauseous, I need to focus: walk through the field to the 7-Eleven, get cigarettes, and get home. A dry-mouth thirst pushes me on. I desperately need a soda.

Warmth spills onto the sidewalk and wraps its radiance around me. I look through an open doorway and see colors splashing like flying paint.

"Hello!" A woman's voice startles me. "Would you like to come in?"

I squint to see an unexpected smile widening on a pleasant face connected to an exceptionally large body. Still unable to stand up straight, I muster a hello, suddenly embarrassed to be caught wearing the sweats that I slept in. I need to get cigarettes, but her wide smile and warm invitation has me looking past her large girth and into the store. The bright colors and the scent of sheep's wool pull me in.

"How long have you been here?" I ask, stepping out of the sunshine. Couldn't be long, I think, because I would have noticed a new store.

"We opened last week," the woman says. "My name

is Carol. My daughter, Shawnee, will be here soon. Come in, come in."

"Nice to meet you, I'm Lee." Funny, my first name is Carol, too, which is good because I'll be able to remember hers. I'm terrible at remembering names.

A young woman enters the store. By the size of her and her pleasant smile, she must be Carol's daughter. She gives her mother a hug.

"This is my daughter, Shawnee." Carol keeps her arm around the woman, and the warmth of their relationship is obvious. An ache wells in my heart and I clutch my flannel shirt and try to remember when my mother might have hugged me like that.

I can't.

"Hi, I'm Lee." My stomach growls and although I'm less nauseous, I don't have the energy to have a conversation about Shawnee's unusual name, so I don't ask.

Shawnee and Carol encourage me to look around while they settle at the old round oak table by the large front window. They knit while I explore the rest of the long narrow store. The shelves explode with tangles of textures and colors. Magenta catches my eye and I pull a skein from its crammed cubby, press it hard to my nose and inhale, exhale...and inhale again, letting the smell take me to a place—I can't quite put my finger on it—a place of comfort long forgotten. For a few minutes, I'm lost in it, and the cigarettes, soda, and sickness disappear.

"We're getting ready for lunch," Carol says. "Would you like something from the deli next door?" I remove the yarn from under my nose when I realize that she's talking to me.

"Uh, no thanks, I've already eaten," I lie.

I don't have enough money. I'm too sick to eat, and my brain is screaming for nicotine. I might scrounge enough change from the bottom of my purse for a soda when I get to the store, but that can wait because I really want to stay here. It's Tuesday. My kids are in school but I don't have to pick them up. During the week they live with their father "so I can get myself together."

Truth is, I'm in more trouble because I'm falling apart without them.

"I've never seen so much beautiful stuff," I say, running both hands up and down each row of perfectly organized yarn in a circular motion, soothing so much more than my cracked fingertips. "I want to touch it all."

"Take your time and look around," Carol says. Shawnee nods her head. "The deli is just next door, we'll be right back." What luck...they've trusted me to be in the store alone. How stupid is that? I steal things.

The cover of a *Knitter's* magazine tossed on the table by the window catches my eye. I sift through page after page of beautiful colors and textures of sweater after sweater. I want to make every one of them and be every girl on every page. I think about how to get the magazine into my purse, but change my mind. Something about stealing from this store feels wrong. Now, that's a first.

I can't leave yet with no one else in the store, and as long as I'm here, the cubbies of comfort call out for one more visit. Then, Carol and Shawnee, along with a friend, shuffle in from the deli next door with enough food to feed an army.

"This is our good friend, Judy," Carol says. "Come and sit with us."

Reluctant to leave the yarn, I join them at the table. Napkins and plastic utensils fly out of the paper bag, followed by sandwich after sandwich. Who's gonna eat all this? I'm surprised when Carol places a giant sandwich with a napkin, fork, potato salad, and a large fountain soda in front of me.

"I hope you like Pepsi," she says. I nod, and although I'm parched from last night's alcohol, I realize that I haven't eaten in days. I'm starving.

"So, Lee, do you knit?"

Hunger and thirst take precedence over speaking. My head shakes up and down while I pack my mouth full, trying to catch the mustard and mayonnaise before it squishes out both sides of my face.

"I learned when I was eight," I mumble while swallowing. "My aunt Barbara taught me."

The conversation between the ladies is knitting chit-chat, and it's all so cozy. Judy is probably thirty-something, absolutely gorgeous, dressed to the nines, and as sweet as Carol and Shawnee. I've never met people like this. A few customers come in while our lunch mess covers the table, but the chaos doesn't seem to faze them. Carol answers knitting questions with a smile, so happy and nice to them all. I would like to be like that, nice to everyone, but I don't think I know how.

I eat everything in front of me. Then, because I can't wait any longer for a cigarette, I stand up.

"Thank you very much for lunch," I say, barely touching Carol's arm. Embarrassed by my inability to pay and the thoughts of stealing still weighing on my mind, I'm ready to get out of here and go home.

"Come back and see us tomorrow," they chorus.

Why? I didn't buy anything. I thought you had to buy something.

"Okay, maybe..." I use my standard response to

anyone who asks me to go somewhere or do something. Not knowing which blender drink will consume me tomorrow keeps me from making promises to show up anywhere. I buy a pack of Marlboros and walk home but something doesn't feel quite right.

Maybe, because, for the first time I can remember, I feel good inside.

The next day, I postpone my drinking routine. Instead, I walk in the direction of the yarn store. Maybe there will be a few new friends to meet and a ball or two of new yarn waiting for me to touch. I sit on the wooden bench outside of the store, eager to soak up the warmth and watch the knitters whose colored strands spill onto the sidewalk.

Smokers hang out here and suddenly Judy squeezes in next to me and lights a cigarette. The bench is full and comfy in the sun.

I don't want anyone to know that my nights consist of drunken self-abuse, rides in police cars, and an occasional institutional lockup, so I ask about her knitting, which fascinates me the same way it did when I was little. It's amazing how you can take two sticks and a piece of string and make something out of it. The longer I stay here, the less time I'll have with the blender and the misery it always brings.

I'm invited to join Carol and Shawnee for lunch again.

After a week or so of daily visits, I overhear Judy telling Shawnee that I don't have a knitting project. "She seems to know a lot," Judy tells her. "She's helped me read my pattern and follow the directions." Carol and her daughter call me in and sit me down at the well-worn table, and I'm shaking inside, sure I must be in some kind of trouble.

"I need a sweater to hang in the shop," Carol says. "My son has been asking for a fisherman's sweater for quite a while. If I give you the yarn and the needles and a pattern, do you think you could make it? It has lots of cables and, of course, I'll pay you to knit it."

"Oh, for sure, yes, I would love to knit a sweater for the store," I answer, trying to hide my desperate eagerness...not an easy task by any means. In my mind, I've just won the lottery.

Night after night, I prop the pattern on my pillow in front of the bedroom window and knit. The drinks on the nightstand go untouched and the sad, sappy songs from the cassette player sit silent. Intently focused on twisting cables, I hardly realize the passing of time. My thoughts drift to a place where I believe that I might be capable of good things, where I might be able to get well, a place where I am a good mother, and while I knit, I find a place where I feel something close to happiness.

I am stunned by what my hands are doing. I thought I would have a hard time figuring out the pattern, but it makes perfect sense to me. Although I loved the motion of knitting, I don't remember making anything useful at the age of eight, but I do remember looking through my mother's knitting books and magazines because I wanted to learn what the words meant. That way, when I watched her knit, I would know what her hands were doing. That's probably why this pattern is making sense.

If nothing else, I am determined. I don't want to disappoint Carol and Shawnee because they believe in me.

Day after day, I work on that sweater at the table where I ate lunch with new friends. I knit next to them on the wooden bench outside the shop, under the same window where I first felt the colors of the sun. I knit at night in my bed, and I keep knitting until it's finished. It is perfect. They told me.

And then they hung it in the window.

part one
Changing

chapter one

Palette of Comfort

"JESUS CHRIST...SON-OF-A-BITCH, God-*damn*-it."
Lightning strikes the front door and my father enters the
house. It hurts to breathe. I need to figure out where to
hide and I need to be fast, like Peter Rabbit, but indeci-
sion nails my feet to the floor. In agonizingly slow motion
I run, but I can't seem to reach my closet fast enough.
His yelling hurts my head.

We have time before dinner is ready. I leave the
closet door open just a sliver so the yelling is muffled, so
I won't have to hear the words.

While I'm crouching on a pile of clothing and toys
in the semi-darkness, friends appear as I call upon them
and we whisper together in our secret language. If I make
myself small enough and press against the wall at the
back of the closet, there's room for us all. Hey...what's this?

Something scratches my leg, and, still adjusting to
the darkness, I can't quite make it out. I'm familiar with
all the things that live here, so I pick it up. When I feel
the prick of wool, heavy and thick, I do know this thing—
it's a sweater my mother made for me. Every winter after
sled rides down the front hill, it would become laden with

clingy little balls of crusty snow. After collecting our wet clothes, she would hang it on the folding rack above the central heater where it would sizzle and hiss as ice bits melted and dripped into the grate covering the hole in the floor where fire lives.

Closing my eyes, I lift the sweater to my face and inhale deeply. The sheep smell takes me to a lime-green pasture brightened by sunshine and summer violets. I stand very still, close enough to imagine the animals' contentment while they move slowly over the pasture carpet that sustains them. Suddenly, from the corner of my eye, I see the dog—it's a shepherd, crouched and focused, dashing and darting, nipping at their heels. The sheep obey and move in sweeping unison—a turn to the right, then a left, then a right again. As they move away, a small sheep remains behind, huddled against the fence.

"Get out of the closet," my sister bosses from her side of the room. The sheep scatter like marbles smacked with a cat's eye. Maybe my brother will play a game with me after dinner. I worry about the little sheep left behind and how he'll find his way home. I smell food—meat loaf and baked potatoes.

The man on the sidewalk is still yelling at his girlfriend while they walk away from the store entrance. Only then do I notice the cashier's direct stare. I'm frozen in the center of the shop with a death grip on three skeins of yarn, one of which is shoved under my nose where I was happily sniffing before the yelling began. I wish my friend Stacie would hurry up and get here. She's been on vacation from the yarn store, where we work together, and today's our day for coffee and shopping.

The riot of color all around reminds me of the task at

hand. I have to decide, after more petting and sniffing, how many of these skeined treasures I will allow myself to take home.

Caribbean blues and canary yellows carry me to crystal waters where ocean beaches hide colored sea glass smoothed by changing tides, and a brilliant orange bird-of-paradise blooms from a cliff nearby. Earthy tones take me to a dry creek bed lined with speckled-brown, weathered rocks. How does one choose their palette of comfort? The addict in me wants it all.

"Hey, there you are!" Stacie walks in. After a quick hug, she joins me in a hunt for new yarns, magazines, needles, books, and anything else we might not have seen before. We touch every skein of yarn and knitted sample in the store for almost an hour, until I buy a skein of lace-weight merino in hues of sky blue and shades of green, enough bright pink fuchsia cotton for a little girl's dress that I have on the design board, five skeins of my favorite Cascade wool in earthy tones to make...well, I'm not sure. It really doesn't matter. I just have to have it.

With knitting bags in hand, we walk across the parking lot to the coffee shop. I spot a vacant table with comfortable-looking chairs outside in the sun near a gurgling fountain, and we sit and knit together for a few minutes before I tell her about the yelling episode she missed, and how it reminded me of my father. She looks concerned as she sips her coffee.

"It's no big deal," I assure her. "I'm over it, but guess what else happened?" Stacie puts her knitting down and, like a good friend, she gives me her full attention. "Remember the story I told you about the yarn store I found when I was a mess, how the owners fed me lunch every day and gave me yarn and needles to make a sweater for the store? And even though I was still drinking and partying at night, knitting that sweater pretty much saved my life?"

"Yeah, I remember you telling me that story one day at work," she says.

"Well, you're not going to believe it." I feel my excitement ramping up. "But just the other day, one of the girls, Judy, from that store…it was called 'Yarn-It,' who I haven't seen in forty years…she hung out on the bench and knit with us…she walked into work and as soon as we recognized each other, we hugged and cried and laughed and I just about died. We talked about trying to find the mom, Carol, and her daughter, Shawnee, and the fisherman sweater that I made for the store, and I told her that I've never forgotten how they all saved my life when they invited me in and treated me like family."

Stacie starts to say something and then pauses. I wonder if she's listening.

"I have something to tell you," she leans forward. "Something that I've never told anyone."

I can't wait to hear. I love gossip and a good story. "What is it?" I ask.

"For my entire childhood, my mother never got out of bed. She was so depressed that she never got out of bed. I had to take care of her almost all the time. I never wanted to be like her, so depressed that I couldn't get out of bed."

I know depression, but not that kind. Stacie looks around to see if anyone is listening and leans a little closer. My knitting falls into my lap, needle stuck in mid-row.

"But there I was, ending up just like her. I spent months in bed. I would stay there every day until three in the afternoon, get up just long enough to fix dinner for my husband and son, read a little, and then go back to bed. I hated myself for being so depressed, so much like her. I finally decided that I needed to find something that would motivate me to get up and out. Being agoraphobic made things worse, but every morning I would force myself to get into my car and drive down the street to this little breakfast place that served the best waffles ever. Every morning I would sit there drinking coffee, reading the paper, and eating. And then I would eat some more. At least I was out of the house, I told myself. As time went on, as you can see, all those waffles caught up with me and I had to find something else to do besides eat.

"It was a Wednesday and I braved the trip to Santa Rosa because I heard about a Sit and Knit group that was happening on Wednesdays at the yarn store. I thought that at least if I was knitting, I wouldn't be eating. When I walked in, I saw only you and one other lady at the table. When I asked about joining the knitting group, you said, 'What group?'"

"I remember that," I interrupt.

"I felt so dumb and embarrassed coming all that way, way out of my comfort zone. There was no group, so I turned around to leave, but you told me to stay, you said that I should stay anyway and knit with you, and you patted the seat next to you at the table." She looks into her cup.

"You talk about how those people saved you so long ago? You paid it forward without even realizing what you were doing. I got out of the house and started coming to knit with you and to have someone to talk to. Who knew I would end up with a job? You were so nice and your invitation gave me a way out of my depression—a way to break the cycle of following in my mother's footsteps. You saved me."

She pulls a tissue out of her purse and apologizes for her tears while I let mine fall through the wrought iron table. I had no idea.

Knitting and working with her, enjoying her bubbly, happy-go-lucky personality and watching her interact with customers, I would have never guessed that she was, at one time, lost and broken and that an invitation to sit and knit would have snowballed into a ticket to mend. We both blow our noses simultaneously.

"Allergies!" We laugh. It's time to go home, and our good-bye hug seems to be a little tighter and last a lot longer.

Processing her story takes a long time as I realize that I actually did something meaningful for someone else. I had shared some of my story and helped another person, and she thanked me. On the drive home, I have time to feel good about myself, something I'm not accustomed to.

Once at home, I'm greeted by yarn on every shelf and basket in the big room upstairs, and I remind myself that it's time to find a place for new purchases. That means that older yarn has to leave the shelf and live in the closet, but opening the door is risky business. I'm never sure just how much treasure pushes against the sliders, waiting to bust out. And, yes, just as I expected, a cascade of color bounces out of the closet.

One by one I lift the yarn to my nose and close my eyes, each inhalation painting scene after brightly colored scene. As I sit in my closet on my palette of comfort, nothing hurts my head.

chapter two

The Pearl and the Bear

I SMELL POPCORN AND cotton candy long before I see the Ferris wheel. As soon as the ticket taker rolls a red stamp onto the back of my hand, I push through the only-one-person-at-a-time-can-get-through revolving wrought iron gate. A bus drops off a few dozen nine- or ten-year-olds, all wearing the same blue T-shirts. A gate at the back of the bus lowers a wheelchair and I'm glad they'll be getting in line behind me, because I'm in a hurry—my first entry into the county fair is waiting.

The pavilion is gigantic. Never have I seen so many beautiful things in one place. Quilts in a multitude of colors and patterns hang from ceiling rafters. I imagine floating beds covered in cotton comforters and I want to touch them all, but rules are rules. We're not allowed to touch the displays and staff members keep a watchful eye. Somehow able to contain my excitement, I begin a slow, methodical procession around the perimeter of the inside of the building. My very first afghan is in here somewhere.

While intently inspecting every knitted, crocheted, sewn, beaded, braided, and hooked item, I see the same name tag on three sweaters, a pair of pink slippers, four hats, two pairs of gloves, and a doll—all displaying a first place blue ribbon. Who is this person? How does one person knit all these things? I thought you could only enter one thing, so I search out a staff member and she explains about categories. Next year, I'll read the submission guidelines. But, for now, it's all so comfortable, all the colors and all the handiwork, all in one place. I had no idea that all of these people sit home at night and make things with their hands. I get to be a part of it; I get to belong to a community that I never knew about.

I still don't see my afghan and anxiety kicks in. Where is it? Maybe somebody took it. People steal things. It must be in here somewhere.

A small group gathers and I stop my search long enough to see why. A pull from a spinner's bag brings forth a stretch of white woolly roving and while others watch her hands pinch, pull, and spin, I'm mesmerized more by the back-and-forth motion of her feet.

"I've always wanted to spin," I tell her, "but I know I'll become addicted and then I'll have a ton of yarn with no time to knit."

"I know exactly what you mean, I have a room full at home." She sees my knitting poking out of my bag. "Why don't you stay at the table with us for a while and knit?" I always carry my knitting because I never know when I might need it.

"I'll come back after I find my afghan."

A procession of onlookers bunches up in front of the next display and my impatience grows. "Excuse me, excuse me...please."

I'm trying not to push, but discomfort in a crowded room keeps me needing to move. How rude to block the flow of traffic. As long as I'm stuck here, I might as well have a look. I inch my way into the center of the pileup and see an enormous cream-colored Aran afghan with intricate cables twisting this way and that over the entire surface, draped nicely over a wicker chest of drawers. It looks strangely familiar, similar, no—exactly like the one I knit. In fact, my name is on the card, and attached to it is a shiny, blue, first place ribbon.

"It's mine," I yell. "I won first place! Are you kidding? I won a blue ribbon."

A few onlookers applaud. Not at all embarrassed at my outburst, I'm elated. As soon as the group moves on, I linger just within earshot to hear what anyone else passing by might say about my winning prize.

At the next display, I squeeze myself in next to a young girl, maybe in her twenties. When I glance her way, she looks like she's ready to cry. Why would anybody cry at the fair?

She's staring at a large crocheted bear, all gussied up in a frilly pink dress, striped leggings, and a floppy hat covering everything except her two-toned ears. She has a basket of rainbow-colored crocheted flowers attached to her right paw and little Mary Jane shoes on her brown bear feet. The upside-down, Y-shaped embroidered nose gives a downturn to her mouth and a sad look, much like the one on the face of the girl standing next to me. Perhaps she doesn't know that the blue ribbon on the table belongs to the bear.

"Is that yours?" I ask.

"It is," she answers, wiping at her eyes with the cuff of her sweater. "I wasn't sure if I should enter it."

"She's adorable, and you won a blue ribbon!" I congratulate her, but something is wrong. "Why wouldn't you enter it?" She digs the toe of her shoe into the linoleum floor and twists it, grinding at something that I can't see.

"Well," she pauses. "It's for my sister. Today is her birthday."

"Oh, I'm sure she won't mind getting her present a little late, especially with a blue ribbon attached!"

I don't know why she's so upset, but I see that she's ready to fall apart. On the way in earlier, I had noticed a wooden bench in the sunshine in front of the pavilion.

"Do you want to go sit outside for a while?" I ask. She hesitates. "Come on. Let's go outside. It's too crowded in here right now, anyway."

"Okay." She tells me her name is Sandie.

We sit in the sun for a few minutes and take in the sights and sounds of the fair. I smell cinnamon, which means funnel cakes, that's for sure.

"I never expected a ribbon." She shuffles both feet back and forth in the dirt. I sit quietly on the bench in the warmth of the sun and contemplate knitting.

"I was hoping for one," I say. "I've never won anything."

"I entered this bear for my little sister. We knew she was sick and the doctor said she only had weeks, not months or years. I wanted to make a special bear to be buried with her, but I couldn't bring myself to make it. I thought if I put it off, then maybe my baby sister wouldn't die."

"Oh, wow, I'm so sorry." My blue ribbon elation vanishes along with the rest of the fair.

"She died. It was so hard to crochet through the tears and I had to hurry, so I made up a pattern and crocheted from my head. It was small enough to fit in the palm of her hand, and I stuffed it, but I thought it needed something more...something special. I searched the house and then I found my grandmother's heart-shaped pendant necklace. A pearl from the pendant would be perfect, I thought, so I stuffed the tiny bear with it and I had to hurry to get it there on time. I barely made it. I had to hand it over to the funeral director. I was so upset because I wanted to give it to her myself."

Tears rim my eyes.

"It took a long time for me to crochet again. I beat myself up pretty bad, thinking I should've made that bear for her before she died, thinking it might have made her happy. I put my hooks away and all my yarn. Every time I thought about crocheting, the memories made me so sad. And then a friend said that maybe I should make another bear...a healing bear. 'Make a healing one for yourself,' she said. I hadn't thought of that."

"So, you made the one inside?"

"Yeah, it helped to think that I was making a healing bear, it helped me a lot. Ever since then, I haven't been able to put my hook down."

"She's perfect. Let's go back inside and look at our ribbons."

Music and barkers beckon fairgoers to ride the rides, and shrieks of fear or fun, I'm not sure which, waft into the pavilion. I'm surprised to see some of the teens in the blue T-shirts still milling about the hall; I imagine that the rides would be more fun than a roomful of crafts. Sandie and I tool around together for another half hour, critiquing and admiring everything, especially our winning entries. I pause at the spinning station for a minute and Sandie says she'll be right back.

"Okay, see you in a few." I sit in a folding chair and

watch the spinners spin.

A bit of a ruckus draws my attention to the display where Sandie's bear lives. A group of the blue-shirted teens rally around a wheelchair, and the girl strapped into it is having some kind of a fit.

What the heck is going on? I make my way over to the display.

"It's her birthday." Sandie looks up at me, fighting tears. The bear is snuggled in the arms of the girl in the wheelchair. "I asked the staff and they said I could give it to her."

As we leave the pavilion, I look at Sandie. "Why would you want to give away something so special to someone you don't even know?"

"It's a healing bear," she says.

chapter three

Healing Sticks

PAUSING FOR A FEW minutes on the sidewalk in the morning sun leaves me anxious and eager with anticipation. Today, my key turns easily in the lock, releasing the rich scent of bamboo, ebony, and birch. Book bindings line up in vertical stripes on pristine white shelves and the scent of sheep wool spun into colorful balls is as comforting to me as a box of Crayola crayons is to a kid in kindergarten. It's been years since Carol and Shawnee, and this is my first job in a real yarn store.

Five minutes into my shift, with morning duties accomplished, I park myself in the comfy queen's chair at the table in the back of the store and prepare for the day. A deep sigh lessens my anxiety as I reach into my tapestry bag and pull out my project: a pair of self-striping socks. The squeaky door hinge signals the arrival of a customer the minute my socks land on the table. Darn. I didn't get to knit a single stitch.

"Good morning. If there's anything I can help you find, let me know." This is my usual greeting for everybody, including all the new knitters who inundate me with questions. I hope the irritation in my voice goes unnoticed; I don't want the first customer of the day to think that I'm a grouch, but I am, until I knit a few rows.

The bald head I notice fascinates and intrigues me. The grungy (Is it paint?) bib overall shorts, sneakers, slouched socks, faded green T-shirt, and flat chest leaves me unsure if she's a he or he's a she. It doesn't matter really, but the wrong gender slipping off my tongue would cause severe embarrassment. Incredulously, it happened to me twice—someone called me sir and the expletives I spewed weren't appropriate, even at a gas station.

"I need help." Her smile is genuine but tired. My curiosity satisfied, I un-grouch and relax.

"What can I help you with?" She appears to be only a few years older than I am, but it's hard to tell.

"I just had a treatment, so I don't have much time until I get sick, so could you look at this?" She pulls her bag off her shoulder.

"You had what?"

"Treatment. Chemo. I'm having treatment for breast cancer." She rubs her flat chest.

I want to know everything. How does it feel to have no breasts? Does the chemo hurt? How sick do you get? Did you find a lump? How often did you check? No reconstruction? But I can't just come out and ask. I'm thinking about how devastated I would or wouldn't be without a chest, when she tosses her knitting bag on the table.

"I just had one of my last few rounds. I only get a few days off from work and my boss is being a total pain in the ass about it." She rolls her eyes up into their lids with no brows or lashes. "I figured I'd have some time to knit, but I'm stuck, so that's why I'm here."

"Sit down, let's take a look. What kind of work do you do?" I ask.

"I cut fish heads."

I'm a little kid in the front yard. It's almost dark. The electric cord from the clip-on lamp that stretches across the front yard trips me while my father cuts the head off of a five-foot swordfish. I worry that the sawhorses holding the thin sheet of plywood won't have the strength to last the hours it will take to clean the fish. My father yells at me for tripping over the wire.

"Salmon heads." She snaps me out of my daydream.

"Oh." I decide not to pass judgment on her job; somebody has to cut fish. Many months go by before I learn that cutting fish heads is a job description with the Department of Fish and Game, explaining her fish fascination and subsequent tattoo.

From her hobo bag, she produces a gorgeous, almost finished vest, perfectly knit on size two needles with Noro sock yarn in shades of ocean blue, seaweed green, and forest brown. Mystery surrounds the reasoning behind her asking for help because it appears that her knitting is perfect. While waiting for her question, and oohing and ahhing over the vest, I try not to stare at her bald head, which I really want to touch.

"Can you show me how to sew up the side seams and fix this little hole in the neck here? I already started it, but I'm not sure if I'm doing it correctly." Scrutinizing every stitch, turning and tossing the vest, the perfectionist in her resonates with me and I like her already. With anticipation and expectation she hands me the vest and after looking it over for a quick second, I pass it back. The yarn needle is already threaded and stuck partially up the side.

"Show me how you were sewing the seam."

She places the needle properly, and sends it through the two horizontal bars that lay one stitch in from the edge, and after a short pull, dives back into the other side lifting the two bars and drawing the yarn through. I watch her perform a perfect mattress stitch.

"You don't need my help, this is perfect. How long have you been knitting?"

"This is my first real project from a pattern. I bought the book and the yarn and I really want to wear it, so I just made it. Besides, I need something to do while getting the chemo. A lot of patients knit while they wait."

"Are you serious? This is awesome." Her obvious intelligence leaves me wishing I had chosen a more educated response. "Let's look at your pattern."

Clearly excited, she explains in great detail her take on the directions, how she modified the numbers to ensure a perfect fit. Her ability to understand the construction of a garment and to do the math impresses me, to say the least.

We spend the next half hour (which is not nearly enough time) discussing knitting lingo without wordy explanations. SSKs, K2togs, and M1s slip easily into her comprehensive mathematical right brain, allowing me a refreshing break from the technically challenged needy knitters, often the norm in the store.

A bright red yarn will stand out in clear contrast to the blues, greens, and browns of her vest. A practice duplicate stitch before attempting to fix a hole is a good idea so I thread a needle with it while she watches with great interest.

"Pull the yarn up from underneath at the base of a stitch and pull it through to the front; then, following the line of the yarn behind the stitch already there, insert the needle from right to left behind and across the top of the 'V' and take the yarn down through the same hole you came up from. See? You make a new stitch that lives directly over the one that was already there."

"It's much easier to learn when you watch someone do it. I still find it difficult to follow the directions from a book."

She seems somewhat proper and her quiet, electric enthusiasm is new to me. Oblivious to anything but the task at hand, she picks up the needle and threads it with her Noro. In minutes, the tiny hole in the neck of her vest disappears, and after a short tutorial, meticulously tucked ends are nowhere to be found.

"What a great job!" I brag for both of us.

"I have to go now. I'm not feeling very well. I think I can finish up the rest. Thank you for your help, I'll come back again when I can."

"Oh, okay, you're welcome. Come by anytime, you're a great knitter."

"I will, thanks."

"Hey, what's your name?" I didn't think to ask, I usually don't, because I never remember anyway.

Roxanne and her cancer walk out the door.

A week later, on a very warm morning, Roxanne returns with a broad smile stretched across her face. Even from my chair at the back of the store, I see her blue eyes sparkle. Seeing her bouncy and giggly, I assume she has good news. It takes me a minute to realize that she is wearing the vest *and* a pair of woolly hand warmers and I have to laugh because it must be a hundred-and-one degrees outside, way too hot to be wearing a wool vest and hand warmers and enjoying it.

"Well, look at you. Look what you made! Doesn't it itch? No way would I even think about wearing Noro wool next to my bare skin."

"Not itchy at all," she says. "And look, I made these."
She sticks both hands out in front of my face.

"Wow, these are awesome." I inspect her work. A pair
of gray and black fingerless gloves in chunky Noro cover
a large portion of both hands, leaving only her fingertips
and elbows exposed. "I bet they're keeping you toasty
warm on such a cold day." She scowls, my sarcasm noted
and accepted.

"I brought something else I want you to look at." We
exchange excitement over a new pattern book. I can tell
that she's eager to start a new project but I can't control
my curiosity any longer and I ask about her cancer.

"Medications keep changing and some are making
me nuts, I can't sleep," she says, "and I'm always tired."
She shares some of her story, how reconstruction doesn't
interest her, but I think she's more comfortable talking
about knitting. After an hour and a half, she leaves the
store with a new bag of yarn slung over her shoulder and
I'm sure I see a little bounce in her step on the way out.

Knitters are drawn together by their common excitement and the thrill of discovering anything and everything related to knitting. Books, yarn, needles, and
notions—all of it enthralls us. I spent years knitting for
the fair, honing my skills, shooting for that best-in-show
ribbon. My accomplishments gave me incentive to keep
going. Working in a yarn shop gives me a chance to pass
on what I learned and to help others.

I knew I'd see Roxanne again because she was definitely excited by everything there is to know about knitting. I didn't expect to see her every week.

Roxanne asks a lot of questions, which, for some
reason, doesn't bother me. Many customers push the
question limit over my allotted "suck my brains out"

comfort zone, and I can get a little testy with them. Especially annoying are the ones who ask a question, get an answer, and then argue with me. Roxanne pays attention and soaks up knowledge like a sponge.

Our friendship grows. She finishes her treatments and we don't talk about cancer. Instead, we talk about knitting and her bitchy boss and fish. I learn a lot about cutting fish heads. Roxanne grills me for knitting know-how, and her work continues to amaze me.

One time, she came in wearing a beautifully knit, fire-engine red wool hat tied under her chin, complete with a pair of devil horns stitched on top.

"What?" she asked. "It's a devil hat. Don't you like it?"

"It's very cool. Did you make it?"

"Yes, I did, and you want to see something?" Roxanne removes her hat and I think I see a few hairs, too sparse to tell what color. She rubs her hand back and forth over the top of her head to fluff them up.

"Wow, can I touch it?" She leans over slightly and tips her head forward so I can feel the small patch of light brown fuzz. "I love your hat, but I can't believe you're wearing a wool hat in this heat. You really made it?"

"Yes, I made it a while back. The pattern was an easy one to follow...and my head is cold!"

Roxanne starts to come to the store's knitting group. Once quiet, reserved, shy, and seemingly in need of friendship, we all watch her blossom. Not only is she a crazy good knitter, she starts to design and write her own patterns. Convincing her to submit some of them for publication is a challenge, but, in the end, my persistence pays off.

The day comes when she bounces in with good news.

Another one of her patterns has been accepted for publication. And she bought a spinning wheel and started spinning her own yarn. She painted the wheel, shared her talents with online knitting and spinning groups, and she feels better every day while she makes things with her hands.

Her work schedule keeps her away for several months, and the next time we see her, she's wearing a sheep fleece around her neck like a mink coat. Roxanne...it's July in California.

I learned much more from her than I gave in knitting instruction. After a treatment, as sick as she was, she would come to knit, or ask questions about a new technique, or sometimes just to talk. I was taken by her strength and desire to keep knitting to feel better. Her knitting skills soared and, as her hair grew, so did her confidence.

It's no surprise she beat the cancer.

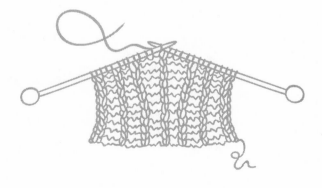

part two
Overcoming

chapter four

Circles

SEVEN YOUNG GIRLS FILL the table at our first beginning knitting class. Alicia, Katie, Lexi, Stephanie, Marsha, Rosie, and Tessa, or is it Theresa? I don't know why I bother to ask their names because I'll never remember them.

"The best way to begin is to take the end from the middle." It makes perfect sense to me, but judging from the blank stares and bulging eyeballs in the room, I have to assume that none of these teens are aware of this timely trick. Filled with anticipation, we begin. "First, pinch your fingers together like this." My thumb and index finger snap open and closed like the jaws of an alligator. "Then insert them into the center of the ball and say 'Abracadabra' while rooting around for anything that feels like the end of the yarn." I get lucky—nice way to begin my first class—and pull a crinkled end from the center of the ball.

"I got it!" Katie produces the same crinkly end. Three others in the group pop out a small wad of yarn, but the end is visible, so we can make it work. Lexi and Stephanie, in a gallant effort, rip out half of the ball's guts into a tangled mess, not unlike a pile of silly string.

"It's okay," I tell them. "We can fix it." Alicia gives up completely and fires the ball across the table.

"I can't do this," she whines. Something about her reminds me of me.

"If the end eludes your magic fingers," I explain, "you can take the label off and use the yarn from the outside of the ball." I retrieve the yarn from the floor on the other side of the table and hand it back to Alicia. I have no doubt that she'll be the one to try my patience.

I've found, over the years, that it's better to teach newbies how to knit first, and then cast on. I've already prepared seven sets of needles with twenty-five stitches in seven different colors and I pass them out around the table.

"What about this yarn?" Katie asks.

"You get to take that yarn home. It was a practice ball just to find the end." Smiles all around, except Alicia, who still looks mad.

"Has anyone ever knit before?"

"My grandmother taught me when I was little," Tessa says, "but I don't remember a thing."

"You will. Your fingers have muscle memory. They'll remember the minute you hold the needles." Disbelief furrows her brows. "It's true, you'll remember as soon as you hold the needles." With all seven students casting on, it's time to begin. That's when the question pops up, as I knew it would, because it always does.

"What are we going to make?"

"Nothing." The brat in me pauses. "We're going to learn how to knit." You know how twelve-year-olds make that long, drawn-out whine when things don't go their way? I got seven of those. They come to a beginning class with the notion that they'll be making something spectacular—a scarf, a hat, socks...maybe a baby blanket. And they want to start knitting it right away, right now, right this minute.

"There isn't anything you can't make," I tell them, "but you won't like how it looks until you practice making the stitches. You can't make a three-course dinner until you learn how to cook."

Disappointment shows, but I'm smiling because I know what's coming. I start with Tessa, the one who's knit before, hoping her easy success will motivate the rest.

"Okay, ready? Take the needle and stick it in the first stitch from the front...like this...and make an X." Both my arms wrap around her shoulders while my hands guide her fingers.

"Now...you'll have to let go with your right hand, so you have to figure out a way to hold both needles in your left. Squeeze your thumb and forefinger and let the needles rest on the tips of your other fingers."

She wraps the yarn around the needle and maneuvers it perfectly under the stitch and off the needle. "That's it! See, you do remember. Look at you, in ten seconds, you're a knitter!" Energy bounces off the walls.

"This is so much fun!" Marsha seems pleased with the progress across her first row as I circle around the table.

"Yeah, it's not as hard as I thought it would be," Lexi says.

Alicia, less frustrated, finally settles down and produces several rows of tightly knit stitches.

"Knitting is so much more than making something to wear." I cut through their concentration. "Eventually, the repetitive motion will bring comfort and a calm that's hard to explain until you feel it yourself, but you'll get it if you knit every day. You have to practice. It feels good to make something with your own hands. People will say wow, you made that?" They just look at me. Twelve-year-olds are such skeptics.

"Arrrggggg..." All of a sudden, Alicia loses it, and rips and pulls at her knitting. By the time I get to her, the needles and yarn are on the floor and her head is crunched into the crook of her arm.

"What happened?"

"I don't know. I can't do anything right." When she lifts her head, her glasses, taped at the bridge of her nose, are crooked and broken. It's hard not to notice her ears sticking straight out from the side of her head.

"Don't worry," I tell her, "there isn't anything that can't be fixed." She straightens her glasses while I get her back on the needles and ready to knit again. I don't think she cares and I don't know why I'm trying so hard, but I'm not giving up.

Stephanie's mother arrives, signaling the end of class. While the girls pack up, I remind them to knit a little bit every day, and tell them if they practice, next week we'll bind off, cast on, and learn to purl. I see a few smiles on the way out. Relieved to have made it through our first class, I plop myself down at the empty table.

I always knew I would be a good knitter; it was just something I knew as soon as I learned to do it. Knitting was the only thing I ever knew I would do well, despite all of the self-doubt in every other aspect of my life. I was determined to be the best knitter, so I practiced...a lot. But teaching wasn't on my to-do list. The opportunity arose and out of necessity, I took it. I taught the beginners, the ones nobody else wanted. The kids are my favorites, reminding me of myself, and the magic I found in the sticks and string when I first learned, fascinated by the process of wrapping yarn around a needle and making something from almost nothing. It's electric for me—to see the light go on in a new knitter's head when they suddenly get it. It's a big part of what keeps me teaching.

The girls arrive for their second class. Some have a few inches of knitting to show off and I can see how proud they are, even though the pieces are riddled with holes.

"Holes are what you should have," I tell them. "You need to make mistakes, in order to learn how to fix them."

While I work around the table, the girls take to the lessons easily, all except Alicia, and I'm not surprised. She appears sullen and moody, and I sit down next to her.

"My dad's coming home soon," she announces out of the blue, while she fishes a mess of tangled yarn from her bag. She hands the needles to me and I turn the mess back into a reasonable facsimile of a knitted piece of fabric; at least for now it's something she can knit on.

"Has he been away?" If we talk about something besides knitting, maybe I can get her to relax enough so she can get herself out of the grip.

"Yeah, he made three hundred dollars, and so he can come home now." She knits a few stitches without a fuss. I don't want to pry, well, yes I do, but more importantly, I want her to keep knitting.

"Do you have a good time with your dad when he comes home?"

"Yes. I love my dad." She doesn't raise her eyes from her knitting. "I live with him and my grandpa." One sentence at a time, she concentrates and makes one stitch after another. She pulls too hard on the yarn and I tell her she has to loosen up.

"Do you have any brothers or sisters?" I ask.

"Twelve," she answers, and makes a very tight stitch, one she can't maneuver off the needle.

"You have twelve kids in your family?" Rosie asks.

"Thirteen, counting me." An audible wow circles the table. I think we're in for a tall tale.

"They're all in foster homes. I have a little sister who got adopted out. She's five." She pulls harder on the yarn.

"*None* of them lives with your mother?" I want to take it back as soon as the words fall out of my mouth.

"No, my mom does drugs." She continues to try to knit, pulling harder. Stitch after stitch. "She smokes..."

"Crack?" I ask. I think it's a good time to go into my why-it's-not-good-to-do-drugs spiel, but Alicia keeps talking.

"Yeah, I keep telling her to stop, but she says she can't. That's why I live with my dad, and when he goes away, I have my grandpa, but he sits in front of the TV all day and watches the news. Grandpas are boring."

I don't know what to say or how to steer the conversation toward something positive. "Yeah, grandpas can be pretty boring." I need time to think.

"When I was in school they used to call me 'Four Eyes'—they even called me a bitch." She leans forward when she says the word, "bitch," and then pushes her glasses back up the bridge of her nose.

"That is so not nice," I tell her. The other girls are

quiet. I give a brief sermon on how sad it is that some kids must be very unhappy, so unhappy that they would be mean to other kids.

"Alicia, look at you, you're knitting, you're doing it... I'm really proud of you." I fix the mess on her needles. The class knits in silence for a few minutes.

"What do you think about when you're knitting?" I ask, to break the silence.

"Nothing." Alicia says. Perfect. This is the answer I want. I want to tell her that knitting opens a hole of nothing so big that all your dreams and wishes and good things live there, and no hurt goes there when you knit.

"If you had one wish, or something that you wanted, what would it be?" I don't know why I ask her, but it's probably the mother in me who wants to take care of her.

"A phone."

"You don't have a phone at your house?" Marsha asks.

"Well, no, my mother lives far away and it costs too much to call her. If I had a phone, I would call my little sister and my mother. How long do I have to knit for?"

I can tell she's done. In trying to open her up, I probably pushed too far.

"You can stop anytime you want." She pulls her sweatshirt over her face and stretches both sleeves long enough to cover her hands and then twists them in knots. It's time to go. Class is over. Her knitting is much better than I expected.

I'm shocked when the owner tells me later that the store is closing. How I hate change. I have a month to buy up all the yarn I can get my hands on and let my regulars know that I won't be moving to the new place. Now what am I supposed to do?

It's hard to pack all of my knitted things from the walls, shelves, and hangers. They were a big part of the "me" that lived in the store. I'll miss my friends, the yarn, and the teaching. I wonder a lot about my students and if they're still knitting. I hope so.

Have you ever noticed when things go almost all the way wrong, something will happen that will turn your world around? In the last days before the shop closes its doors, we have an unusually large gathering for our Wednesday knit-along club, and one of the knitters offers me a free room for me to meet with students. It's in the back of her store near the mall on the other side of town. I won't have a yarn store to work in, but at least I can still teach classes.

Occasionally, Alicia's father will drop her off at the mall and she'll come through the store to the classroom in the back to say hi. Today, when I ask about her knitting, I get the usual response.

"I'm not gonna carry it around with me at the mall."

I wonder if she really does knit, but today I won't push because I have a new class of beginners in session. We're just getting started, and one of the girls is having trouble finding the end of the yarn. Alicia walks right over to her and yanks the yarn from her hand.

"Here, let me show you. First, you have to find the end in the middle...like this...and if you can't find it," she explains while digging into the center of the ball, "you can take the label off and use the yarn from the outside." Alicia tosses the new girl the ball with the curly end exposed, having pulled it from the center perfectly.

chapter five

Ewe and Me

THE STINGING COLD BITES into me. Careful, now—
one wrong step and I'm a snowball rolling down the slippery driveway. I wouldn't want to drop the freshly painted
wooden sign that I made for Martha, the owner at Ewe
and Me, to replace the old sign at the yarn shop where
I work. After a hefty pull, the ice releases its grip on the
car door. With the sign safely on the back seat, I turn my
attention to the windshield, which I would rather hose,
but I know better, so I scrape a frosty circle, just enough
to see through. The familiar scent of burning wood fire
hangs heavy in the air, usually a pleasant smell, but
today it's acrid and burns my nose. Somebody must be
burning green wood, or worse, paper. How dumb.

Warm at last with the car heater blasting, the drive to
work is slippery and I narrowly miss plowing into a dirty
snowdrift piled high at the side of the road. Although the
store owner's friend Sadie spends hours knitting alone in
her car, I'm surprised to see her wagon in the driveway
in front of the yarn shop; it's much too cold for her to sit
in the car, and besides, it's covered with snow.

A bit of a yarn hoarder, Sadie collects scraps and odd

balls of yarn and stores them in her old wood-paneled station wagon. Papers, cups, straws, and other evidence of fast food litter the floorboards along with her treasure trove of yarn. She drives around town with her view impeded by the mile-high piles occupying every available empty space. Rather unkempt and reclusive, she lives alone. Making friends proves difficult for her, but her need (dare I say addiction?) for yarn gives way to visiting yarn stores on a regular basis. At Ewe and Me, she's always invited to stay and knit, but most of the time she declines, although she comes in often to shop. We worry about her impaired vision and the growing mound of junk in her wagon.

I bang my elbow on the door to the store.

"Oh, thank you," Martha pats me on the shoulder. "The sign is divine."

I hang it on the empty nail next to the front door and then close the door quickly to keep the chilly air out. Martha returns to the table and offers me a cup of tea. By the look on her face, I sense something is wrong.

"What's going on?"

Sadie has her head down and her eyes closed. "Last night, I hauled in some wood, like I always do, and started a fire." She speaks slowly, as if in some sort of stupor. "It was so cold that I put a few more logs on. A few more than usual to get it roaring. I pulled my rocking chair close to warm me up while I knit there, like I always do, with Sampson curled up on the hearth."

"Who's Sampson?"

"He's my cat." She doesn't look up.

"I was telling him last night, how I needed to organize some of the tangled mess from the baskets of yarn on the floor around my chair. I told him I'd be right back after I

33

found some scissors. He just stretched and curled back up into a ball, like he always does when I talk to him."

"Sounds like a nice warm place to hang out." I don't think Sadie hears me.

"I spent hours clipping yarn ends, making neat little balls. You know how I treasure every little piece, no matter how small. I didn't want to get up and get a wastebasket, so I tossed the tiny clipped ends into the fireplace. And then...oh my God."

I want to ask what happened, but Martha gives me a look that says be quiet. The teapot whistles from the back room. Martha brings another cup of steaming tea and glances my way. I nod no thanks. She places it in front of Sadie.

"As soon as I realized that I'd thrown the ball into the fire instead of the tail end, my holler sent Sampson skittering off the hearth. I tried to retrieve the little ball by pulling it out by its tail, but it was too late. It was already on fire."

It must have been acrylic. Acrylic burns.

"It came rolling out and landed on the rug at my feet. It dripped fire onto the rug and I stomped on it, but my slippers started to melt. I tried to remember what you're supposed to do...it all happened so fast. Flames came at the legs of my chair and my baskets started to burn. I ran as fast as I could into the kitchen for a pan of water, but by the time I got back, the fire had grown so big that my rocking chair had turned into a red-hot skeleton. I threw the whole pan at it. What was I supposed to do? I couldn't think." Sadie lifts her head off the table with her eyes full of terror. "Oh yes, get the phone. Call 911. I wanted to get more water, but the fire was too big. All I could do was stand there and watch. As soon as I heard the sirens, I knew I had to leave. I was so scared and I didn't know where Sampson was."

Sadie reaches for the box of tissues. Martha pat-pats her shoulder. I can't speak because the adrenaline brought on by the fire that I purposefully set years ago is now flowing through every part of me.

"As soon as I ran out the front door, the frozen air hit me like a slap in the face. It was so cold, I considered going back in for a jacket, or at least one of my sweaters, but it was already too late. Thank God Sampson was in the neighbor's yard. When I called to him, he came running, and then we sat in my car and watched our house burn down." The tissues wad up on the table.

"Sadie came here last night," Martha says. Sampson stretches his way down the carpeted steps from the loft upstairs.

"I'm so glad you're okay." My words feel hollow. I don't think she's okay. I know about fire.

With her limited resources, Sadie has nowhere to go. She spends the next few months living with Martha in the loft over the shop. Every day she searches through newspapers trying to find a place of her own. Martha gives her a job in the store and takes samples off the shelves for her to wear. Sadie wears them reluctantly, she tells me, because they are so special. Customers bring clothes, food, and toiletries. During the day, Sadie helps me run the store and knits with yarn from her car. The trove of trash finally finds its way to the garbage can on the sidewalk down the street. Sadie makes friends. Friends to knit with, share stories with, and heal with. She tries for months to find a place to live.

Early for my shift one morning, I find Martha and Sadie sitting at the table, very excited about something.

"We were waiting for you," Sadie says.

"What's going on?" The two of them look goofy happy.

"Sadie has good news," Martha says.

"I got some money that I didn't know was coming." I've never seen Sadie this animated. "And I bought a house!"

"Yeah, how cool is that? Wait...does that mean you're leaving? Where is it?"

"I'll only be four hours away. You can always come and visit."

"But we'll miss you!" I'm happy for her, and even though she and Martha are friends, I know it's been hard for the two of them living in the small loft together. Sadie's already packed.

"Thank you for everything." She hugs us both, seemingly in a big hurry to leave, probably so we won't see her cry.

"Come back and visit," I say. Martha and I stand on the front stoop.

"I'll call you when I get all settled in."

"I hope she buys a new car," I tell Martha, and although we're sad to see her go, we both crack up at the sight of her old wagon tooling down the road, as full as it's ever been.

Business is summertime slow. When Martha calls me into the back room, I'm pretty sure I already know what she's going to tell me. I've been thinking about a change of pace, anyway. Finding a new job won't be too difficult; I could teach classes if nothing else.

"I'm going to have to give up the shop." Martha is crying. "The owners sold the building and I have to move." This is not the news I was prepared for.

"When? What about the store? Where will you go?"

"I have enough time to sell off the inventory, and then I'll have to stay with my sister until I figure out what to do. This yarn shop has been my forever dream, I just can't believe it." Martha is pacing and wringing her hands. "I need to tell Sadie."

"Let's go see her, it's not that far." It hurts to see Martha so distressed.

For the last few months, Sadie has stayed in touch. She sent us a letter describing her new house and how she had her hands full with the addition of a large sunroom off the entire front. "A beautiful space for knitting and relaxing," she wrote, and invited us to come up. "It will be a gorgeous room."

With the inventory gone, Martha and I make the trip together. Martha wants to tell Sadie about losing the store in person.

After tears and hugs and tea, we reminisce about Ewe and Me. Martha tells Sadie that her sister isn't the ideal roommate and that she's looking for a place to open another store. Despite having to give Sadie the bad news about closing the store, it's a wonderful visit.

When I arrive home, Sadie surprises me with a phone call and lets me in on her plan. "Something I've been working on for quite a while," she says.

I can hardly contain myself. "She'll love it," I say to Sadie.

Over the next few months, Sadie reknits every sweater and scarf that Martha had given her from the shelves of the shop, and when she has them finished, invites us for another visit. I tell Martha I can't make it, but that she should go. (I know what the surprise is.) Happy to take a break from her sister, Martha makes the drive.

"Oh my," Martha cries out as Sadie opens the sunroom doors. "You've got quite a collection of yarns here...and look at all of the books...and needles. Sadie, it looks as though you have enough stuff to open a yarn shop!"

And then she notices the wooden sign propped up against the wall behind her. It's lovely, freshly painted... familiar. "Ewe and Me."

Sadie holds up the sign and raises both brows, a question with no words.

"Don't you think it's time to move out of your sister's place?" she asks.

Sampson stretches and curls himself up in the warmth of the sun.

chapter six

Pencils in Motion

PENCILS, PENS, STICKY NOTES, dirty coffee cups, and knitting notions litter the oblong table under the front window. Who leaves all this mess for the next employee to clean up? Friday night knitters need etiquette lessons. Now I'm irritated and it's first thing Monday morning, and, of course, a customer is outside waiting to come in. I hope she doesn't need any help and just wants to buy yarn. Putting on my best professional smile, I hurry to the front door.

I dump my smile. Are you kidding, who brings their kid to a yarn store first thing in the morning? He looks to be about six, and it's ten o'clock so how come he isn't in school? Kids tear up knitting stores. Breathe. It's just a kid. Relax.

I unlock the door, welcome them in, and ask if there is anything I can help her find. The little boy hopscotches into the center of the store and puts on his brakes in front of a wall unit crammed with a hundred and twenty-six skeins of Cascade yarn. I know, because I counted them while I straightened and smoothed each and every one.

He begins jumping up and down like a pogo stick

and his little hands flap as fast as hummingbird wings. He just jumps and flaps. I guess he likes the bright colors. I can relate.

His mother looks at me apologetically, and my grumpy melts away. The mess on the table can wait and I ask again if there's anything I can help her find.

"I'm really stuck with this pattern, do you offer help here? I'll be happy to pay for help. I'm new here and I heard about this store from my neighbor."

"Absolutely not, help is what we do here and we're happy to give it for free, and just so you know, solving puzzles is my favorite thing to do." With a relieved sigh, she thanks me.

She's young, probably thirty-something and her perfectly coifed chin-length auburn hair is chisel cut, sleek, and shiny. She pulls a tangle of knitting from a matching paisley tapestry bag.

"Let's see what you've got." I gesture toward the table. "Sorry about the mess." As her blue yarn and bamboo needles emerge, she glances toward her son. The pogo stick has slowed, but his wings are working overtime.

"He has Asperger's," she says. "I'm sorry, I hope it's okay that I brought him, he doesn't go to school yet."

"No problem, don't apologize." I mean it. His mop of carrot curls form ringlets around his green eyes and bounce like little springs. "He's adorable, how old is he?"

"He's six." I was right. He hops over to the table and I'm prepared for a question or a comment or a story, but he doesn't speak.

"Hi Cutie-pie, what's your name?" No answer and no eye contact.

"Will he draw?" I ask, spotting the pencils on the table.

"He loves to draw." She tells me her name is Carla and I introduce myself.

"This is Seth." He grins when he sits down, but doesn't look up when I hand him a pencil and a piece of paper. Content for now, I turn my attention to the knitting help that Carla needs. We spend a few minutes on the pattern directions while Seth scribbles happily and then Carla picks up her needles.

Instantly, as if on cue, Seth lifts his head and fixates his eyes on her hands. Although I have to pay attention to Carla's struggle with her twisted stitch, I'm taken by his excitement. I remember being mesmerized by the motion of my mother and aunt's hands while they knit together on the couch. If I sat very still on the floor in front of them and kept quiet, I could be invisible and they would let me watch.

Seth picks up a second pencil from the center of the table and taps the two together, then twists and turns them much in the same way his mother is manipulating her needles.

"I think he wants to knit."

"I think he does," Carla smiles. "He watches me all the time but I don't think he'll ever be able to learn."

"I don't think there's anyone who can't learn." Her resignation is evident, but it's too early for my sermon on how everyone can do it, so I'll try to convince her another time.

While Carla knits, Seth scoops and twists his pencils and follows me around while I straighten up the table. It's awkward that he doesn't speak, but his little grunts and smiles make me believe that he's having a good time. Carla's knitting is on track, and after a quick glance at her watch, she pushes her chair from the table.

"Thanks for your help, I have to go. I have an appointment that I have to get to."

"It was nice to meet you, Carla, come by anytime if you need help, or if you just want to knit. I'm here every day, and you can always bring Seth along."

"He'll be going to a special school, soon. I'm so excited for him, but nervous at the same time." His face lights up at the mention of school.

"Seth, put the pencils back where you found them," she coaxes. He hides them behind his back, and his eyes open wide as he shakes his head no.

"It's okay. He can keep them, if it's okay with you. I have plenty."

"Thanks...and thanks for your help. I'll be back." Carla pushes Seth gently toward the door.

"See you later, Tiger." I point my index finger at Seth's hand, and, surprisingly, like E.T., his index finger connects with mine. I have a new buddy.

Seth starts school, so I don't get to see him again, but I always ask about him whenever Carla comes in the afternoons to knit.

"Right now he's having a lot of anxiety," she tells me as she pulls a bright blue hat out of her bag, "but he likes his teacher. It's a special class for kids with Asperger's and he's talking more. We got lucky to find such a great place for him."

"Does he stay in school all day?" I can't imagine him sitting still that long.

"No," Carla laughs, as if she's read my mind. "I take him to the mall every morning when most of the stores are closed. He likes to touch every rung of every metal security gate, and I let him run and jump the whole length of the mall and back. He goes wild, but so far, the few early-bird shoppers don't seem to mind. I don't know where else he would get the freedom to run and jump and be himself in public. It tires him out enough so he can go to school in the afternoons. Otherwise, he would be bouncing off the walls."

What fun, running through the mall in the early morning hours. I would have never thought of that.

I don't see Carla or Seth for a while. I always wonder what happens when a customer disappears. Life changes and moves forward, and that's just the way it is, but I still think about them.

The end of summer is near, and business has been painfully slow. While knitting by myself at the table, perfectly chiseled hair and a familiar paisley bag walk past the front window.

"Hey, Carla, long time, no see. How've you been, and how's that little tiger of yours?" Carla barely gets in the door before I barrage her.

"I'm fine, thanks. Sorry it's been so long. We had to move again, no big deal, but it was rough on Seth. He hates change, and although he likes school, he's really nervous about going back in a few weeks. Can you help me again with my knitting? I finished my hat. Seth loves it and he wears it every day."

"Even in this heat?"

"Yeah, and now I'm not sure I should be making him a sweater." We both laugh.

"Of course I'll help, sit." We muse over the stitches and I quickly find her mistake, but this time, instead of fixing it for her, I put it in her hands and explain how she can do it.

"But you make it look so easy."

"Knit a little every day and you'll get it. Your knitting

is perfect, look how well you're doing on this summer sweater." We grin again. "You just have to pay more attention if you don't want to make mistakes, try not to knit when you're too tired."

"Believe me, I try. Knitting keeps me sane. If I didn't have it, I don't know what I'd do."

Carla promises to come back as soon as Seth gets situated in his new school.

A few weeks later, she stops by. The store is busy but a couple of regulars are sitting at the table and they invite her over. I finish at the register and by the time I join them, the ladies are hanging on her every word.

"Wait, tell me what happened. I want to hear." I'm so nosy.

Carla puts her knitting down and starts her story again. "A week after school started, I got a call from Seth's teacher. I was terrified at the thought that something had happened to him, but his teacher quickly assured me that he was all right. She wanted to discuss an issue with some inappropriate behavior. I had to ask her to say it again because I wasn't sure what she meant. When she repeated herself, I just about dropped the phone. When I asked her what behavior, she hesitated so long that I thought I'd have a heart attack. I had no idea what to expect."

"What was he doing?"

"She said that Seth has been 'exhibiting some rather peculiar behavior under his desk,' and that the other children have been whispering, and she's worried that Seth will be teased."

"What was it, Carla?" I think I know.

"Well, when she tried to explain, it sounded like she was telling me that he had his hands in his lap under the desk and he might be...you know...touching himself."

A slight gasp emits from one of the older ladies at the table. "Did she ask him if he had to go to the bathroom?"

"Yeah, she did, and he said no, so I was stumped. It took me a few minutes to pull myself together, and I had to rack my brain and then I knew what it was.

"'You're not going to believe this,' I told his teacher, 'but he finger knits in his lap for comfort when he's stressed. He watches me knit and he makes the motion with his hands, usually with pencils. He knits with his fingers in his lap.'"

Two weeks later, Carla brings Seth into the shop. After a flurry of excitement over the yarn he takes a seat at the table next to me and looks directly into my eyes. As I reach for a piece of paper and a pencil, his voice squeaks out a question. "Will you teach me how to knit?"

part three
Grieving

chapter seven

Tuck in the Ends

VALERIE LEANS IN CLOSE and pushes a green beanie hat in front of my face.

"See this? I don't know what to do about this part, right here. I messed it up and I don't know how to fix it. Can you tell me what I did wrong?"

I take the hat. "Here, let me show you." I wait while she digs through her purse for a tissue and blows her nose.

"Sorry."

Everyone around the table watches me unravel her hat.

I recently met Valerie while shopping at a local yarn store. I don't think we ever stopped talking over each other; we shared so much excitement over yarn and knitting. After combing through the store together, I invited her to join our Tuesday knitting group.

"See? All fixed. You just twisted the stitch when you put it back on the needle."

"Next week, will you show me how to tuck in the ends? I have to hurry and finish it because we're moving."

"What? You're moving?"

She can't leave now. I really like her. She's friendly and outgoing and her blonde hair and blue eyes remind me of myself when I was little.

"I have to go. My husband is taking me and the boys to a Navajo reservation in Arizona. He has work there. But I'll be here next week, okay?"

"Okay, but I don't like making new friends and then having them move away. We'll miss you." The group nods as they pack up their knitting.

"See you next week, then." I give her a hug.

Tuesday group is in full swing and this week we have a newcomer who needs help making a cable. I explain how to read the symbols.

"If it says to C6B, it means the cable is over six stitches. You place three stitches on a cable needle and hold in the back, knit three, and then knit the three from the cable needle. Any time you see the 'B,' the cable will slant to the right, and if you have a C6F, you do the same thing, but put the stitches from the cable needle to the front and the cable will slant to the left. *I'll be right back,*" I tell her. "That's how you can remember. If the symbol has a B, you place the stitches from the cable needle to the back and the cable leans to the right. *I'll be right back.* Get it?" Right. Back. I don't know why I always have to say everything twice, but I do.

She gets it, and I watch while she turns half a row of perfectly executed cables to the back, and the other half to the front.

"Perfect!"

Valerie walks in with a gigantic grin on her face.

"I finished my hat." She drops her bag on the table and fishes through it, tossing needles, a tape measure, and yarn on the table. "Here it is."

Unified "oohs" come from the group. She's knitted a brown and blue stripe around the top and it looks great. "I just need to know how to tuck in all of these ends." She flips the hat inside out and laughs at the mass of blue and green and brown spaghetti.

Melancholy quiets me while I show her how to weave in the ends. I feel like I'm about to lose my best friend.

If it wasn't for knitting, I don't think I would have very many friends. Lots of people say they like me, and I believe them, but I'm not ever sure why. I tell them a lot of things about my past and what I'm doing now, but I rarely let anyone all the way in. My knitting friends say that I've changed and grown, that all of the bad things weren't my fault, that I'm a good person. I hope they know how much that means to me.

It strikes me as odd, when you meet someone, and in an instant, you feel as though you've known them forever. That's how it was when Valerie and I met at the yarn shop.

I wish she wasn't moving away. While she watches me tuck, Valerie tells me that her husband isn't being nice to her and she's not happy. I tell her to make sure to keep knitting because it'll help her through the move and all the things that make her feel bad.

"I already started a blue hat for Tristan's little brother."

Two weeks after she left, I get the message about her father.

"Two weeks after we moved to Arizona, I got a phone call. My father took a gun and shot himself. He's dead and I'm devastated. I feel like I'm floating in a dream and all I can do is knit. Knitting is all I can hold onto to keep from falling completely apart. I don't understand why he did that and no one can tell me. I'm a mess and I need to knit, I need to finish this hat so I can knit something else."

Valerie keeps trying to reach him somehow, too late to save things. The loss breaks her heart and she's too far away, so I tell her to keep knitting. Every time we talk, I tell her to keep knitting.

A year passes.

Valerie is returning to visit family and she wants to know if we're still knitting and can she come on Tuesday. I can't wait to see her, but I worry about what to say. Do we talk about her father?

We meet at the store a few hours early, just the two of us.

Knitting news and excitement comes first, and I tell her that sometimes things turn out badly and we never understand why, and then I tell her what happened to me when I overdosed. They all know my history of addiction. I tell her that it doesn't hurt to die and then I ask about her father.

"Growing up, my dad was the most loveable, sensitive, smart, charismatic, and energetic person I knew. I felt bad because I didn't get to spend much time with him and my mom after moving here to California. He worked so hard, and his health started to deteriorate after a few strokes. He was devastated when he found out that he couldn't ride his Harley with his buddies anymore. I worried a lot when I went back to visit and would always leave feeling so guilty because I couldn't help him more. It was hard for him to accept help from people; it drove my mom nuts. He was stubborn as a mule. He found out that he had a rare genetic disorder and he knew that, at some point, he wouldn't be able to walk.

"I went to the store that day, and when I came home, I could tell that something was wrong. My husband was on the phone. He covered the receiver and told me to get the kids and sit them down with a movie. He hung up the phone when I came upstairs.

"I asked him what happened. He told me my dad took his life. I knew he'd been suffering for a long time, but I didn't know he was in that much pain. I was shocked. Utterly shocked. I lost the best person in my life, the person who raised me, supported me, listened to me, and loved me. My dad was gone. That's when I sent you the message, I couldn't tell just anybody. Somehow, I knew you would be there for me."

I reach my arms around her shoulders and hug her tight.

"You know, after my precious dad left this earth, all I wanted to do was knit. Knitting kept me together for my boys. I knitted booties, scarves, hats, and other things. I donated hats to babies. I gave hats away for shower gifts. I still knit as much as I can."

"And look how far you've come and what a good job you're doing."

"That's because I had a good teacher," she says as she whaps me on the side of my arm.

"Valerie! How are you? Did you move back?" Cathy puts her bag on the table and I see Phyllis and Roxanne on their way over.

"No, I wish," Valerie says. "I'm just here for a visit, but I wanted to come and knit with you guys."

"How are things on the reservation?" Carol asks while the others join us.

"Well...actually, my husband and I got divorced, and I was forced to move. Things were pretty stressful for a while, there were challenges and chaos and financial hardships and all the garbage that goes along with a divorce, but I managed to keep myself together. Someone told me to keep knitting, so I did, and that helped a lot." She whaps me again.

Valerie goes home and I get another message.

"I'm moving back next year to California and we can knit together!"

Like finding something special that you lost, I feel like a little kid with a new best friend. I'm beyond excited.

"Are you still knitting?" Silly question.

"Right now, I'm working on a scarf for each of the boys for winter. It feels good to sit between them on the couch and knit. They rest their heads on my shoulders and tell me that they love watching me. Tristan wants to learn...he already knows how to cast on."

"Well, if he needs any help tucking in the ends, let me know."

chapter eight

Moving On

MY FIRST ATTEMPT AT rehab is not a success.

The intake process allows me to eagerly answer questions about myself. I embellish and dramatize my responses, and am equally practiced at placing blame for my misery on the shoulders of others. Attention from the counselor is much appreciated, but thirty days away from my responsibilities is a hard pill to swallow. Maybe they can fix me quicker, so my kids can come home sooner.

Detox reeks of stale cigarettes and musty paperbacks. I'm not physically sick, not like some of the old men in worn bathrobes, but I'm here, so I take a seat among the others.

For thirty days I do what I'm told and although I'm not able to comprehend a "higher power," I pay attention because the people coming to the meetings look well and happy. Some of their stories sound like mine, most are worse, but every time I hear the word "God" I'm angry because there isn't one. If I have to believe in God to get better, then it's not going to happen here, with these people, but they seem so successful in their happiness.

I see a lady with something familiar. She has a cup

of coffee on the floor and knitting in her hands. I like the looks of that. It reminds me of my mother and the sweaters she knit, and I like the way that makes me feel. Maybe I'll try knitting again someday.

Thirty days and I'm cured. With Antabuse in my system and a head full of dreams for a better me, my friends pick me up at the front door. Free at last, I'm excited to be going home, but it's clear that my friends have other plans. The backseat is filled with alcohol, ready for a party in the cemetery, they tell me. My kids are living with their father. They'll be coming home for the weekend in a few days. I was going to go home and clean the apartment.

"But I can't drink," I whine. "I took Antabuse this morning and it'll make me sick if I drink." How could they do this to me?

"Don't worry," my friend says, "I have pills."

Thirty days down the drain. I swallow a few pills and the party begins.

I read somewhere that when a person is about to die, they instinctively know. What I read is correct. Four days and one-hundred-and-fifty pills later, I know for sure that I am going to die. There are no friends, no party, and neither of my children are here to help me. I don't know what day it is. I wonder where they are. They were here a while ago.

I roll off the couch and crawl across the dirty carpet, somehow managing to pull the phone from the kitchen counter to the floor. With my face hovering inches above it, I pick up the receiver and will my finger to find the nine. I press the button twice and I'm devastated because I'm not sure if I can start over. Hang up and start over. Nine...one...one.

As if my head is underwater, I hear their muffled words, "You better hurry or we'll have to put a tag on her toe." Paramedics bump me down the narrow cement stairway on a gurney and my eyes open to daylight. If I am still in the cemetery having a party, why is it not nighttime? The sirens lull me back into unconsciousness.

Coming out of the darkness, I float with my back pressed against the ceiling. I watch as doctors and nurses urgently poke and prod at the girl on the table below. When they step aside, a doctor pumps his tightly cupped hands vigorously on her ribcage. Odd, I think... the girl looks a lot like me. Is that me?

And then I see shadows lined up three-deep along the walls of a narrow hallway, weaving and bobbing gently side-to-side. I believe I see the face of my grandmother but I can't make out her features clearly, nor the faces of anyone else. As I walk slowly through the corridor, I feel their concern, but I am only interested in the golden light that beams through a crack in the double doors at the end of the hall. It is the warmest, brightest, most wonderful thing I've ever seen. I'm drawn to it and I want to go into it.

As I move forward, shadows pool around me. I feel many hands on my shoulders, gentle yet firm, turning me, and I hear voices murmur and hum. "You have to go back...you have to go back." I am sobbing as I struggle to release their hands because I don't want to turn around; I want to go to the light.

My eyes open and I am sobbing and doctors are hovering over me, calling my name and I am angry because I am back.

I spend the next three weeks in an institution on suicide watch. I don't know why, because I only wanted to get high and I only remember taking the first five pills. I'm sick for a week and a half.

As soon as they let me out, I think it is a good idea to go back to those meetings where happy people go, to the place where I heard that I'm not alone with my problems, where I can get help.

I see Paula there. She reminds me of the lady who drinks coffee and knits. I see her at the same meeting for the next two weeks. On the day I feel well enough, I sit down next to her because I'm drawn to the motion of her hands. I want to tell her that I know how to knit too, but before I get the nerve, she's announced as the speaker for the meeting and she gets up and walks to the front of the room.

"I know you won't believe this—because I don't look old enough—but I've been sober for twenty-two years." The audience laughs. She sets her knitting down and leans against the front desk.

"I started drinking as soon as I was tall enough to reach the liquor cabinet, and it wasn't long before that twelve-ounce glass that my parents thought to be filled with water was actually filled with vodka. No ice, no tonic, no lime. After too many years of the trouble that a quart of vodka a day causes, I'd had enough." Paula tells us a few stories that are so similar to things that had happened to me that I can't believe what I'm hearing. I feel like I know her.

"I found rooms, rooms just like this one, where I was able to find courage, camaraderie, and tools to help me stay sober. My life finally became manageable, and then my worst nightmare happened.

"At 2:00 A.M. on October third, I was awakened to the news that my nineteen-year-old son was dead. He'd been to a party where he'd been drinking and after finding the car keys that his friends tried to hide, he drove himself home. He slammed into a tree in our driveway, forty feet from the front door.

"In my suffocation, I stood in the window and watched my driveway light up like a movie set with police sirens and lights flashing everywhere. There was my son's car, wrapped around a tree and he was trapped inside. Dead. It took them three hours to get him out.

"I'm still not over it. I'll never get over losing my son, but the one thing that I didn't do was pick up a drink."

The audience explodes into applause, and I clap while tears run freely down my cheeks. Wow. I would never be able to handle something like that. I'd go off the deep end.

The meeting concludes with the usual routine. I like the circle and joining hands. I want to believe the part where they say, "Keep coming back—it works." Paula is swarmed by people afterward. Although I'm not sure why, I feel a need to say thank you. I want to ask her how I can get better without the "grace of God," because I don't know what that is. I want to tell her not to feel sad for her son because I know what it feels like to die.

Paula picks up her knitting, and I watch several women follow her to the back of the room. Reluctantly, I decide to leave.

"Do you want to join us?" I stop in the doorway and turn around. Two women are setting up a table next to the coffee station. A girl with arms covered in tattoos and flaming red hair joins them.

"Some of us hang out after the meeting and knit," Paula says, "and you're welcome to stay."

"I used to knit a long time ago, but I haven't picked

it up in years." I weave my way to the back of the room through a row of chairs. I want to ask the girl where she got her tattoos, but mostly, I want to ask Paula how she doesn't drink.

I take a seat next to the table. After the ordeal in the hospital, I'm quieter than usual and I don't want to talk about myself, so I watch and listen as they knit. Paula is almost finished with a long scarf, tan, with cables, and one of the other ladies is making a sock with the tiniest needles I've ever seen. The tattooed girl pulls a baby hat from her purse and begins knitting the minute she sits down. They seem so comfortable and I'm desperate to know how they got better, so I get up the nerve and say something.

"How is it that you can live through such a tragedy and still be okay?" I ask Paula. "And you seem so happy."

"I had to learn how to be happy, and the first step was to stop drinking. I come to meetings to remind myself where I came from. It's people just like those who were here tonight that saved me so many years ago...them and my knitting."

"Amen." The sock knitter says.

"After my son was killed, I went into a state of coma-tose oblivion. All I could do was knit. I couldn't leave my house except to see my therapist once a week and to go to the grocery store. I ate the same frozen dinner every day for almost a year. I knit afghan after afghan, like a robot, day after day. It was the only thing that kept me going, the need to finish a project, give it away, and start another one. I wanted so badly to cry, but I was so numb that I couldn't, which made me even crazier. It wasn't long before I wanted to drown myself again, so I looked up this meeting, and, of course, I brought my knitting with me." She lifts the very long scarf from her lap for me to see.

"It's really beautiful," I say. "I especially love the cables. Do you guys knit here every week?"

"Thanks, we do. A lot of people took an interest in my knitting, so I got permission to stay after and knit with anyone who wants to hang out. What better combination—a meeting and then more healing while we knit? Some of the folks who aren't ready, or able, to share at the meetings will open up when they knit or crochet."

"Amen." The sock lady grimaces as she remounts a dropped stitch.

"You said you knit?" Paula asks.

"My aunt Barbara taught me when I was eight. I don't remember making anything specific, but I do remember how it felt when she handed me the needles and the yarn—the minute I touched it, it was like magic. For the first time in forever I felt like I finally had something that I could be in charge of, and I could sit still long enough so I wasn't getting into trouble. And I knit a sweater for a yarn shop once, a cabled sweater like your scarf."

"How about I bring you some yarn and needles next week and we can see how much you remember?"

"That would be awesome." I feel better than I have in months.

"Here, this is for you." Paula stands and wraps her finished scarf around my neck while the other ladies pack up. I'm speechless while I examine her intricate cables.

"Really, for me?" I find the gesture overwhelming and I want to hug her, so I do. "Thank you."

"See you all next week." Paula has the warmest smile.

As is my habit, I sabotage anything good that comes my way. I don't see Paula or the ladies again. Although I'd like to, I don't believe that I can get better by going to meetings where you have to find God. I'm doomed, I think, so I drink again.

Ten years and many meetings later I find what I need and, through the grace of God, I'm able to stop drinking. And I knit.

I knit and knit. I knit because it allows me to fit into the place inside of myself where I find comfort, and fully engaged, transcend and unsnarl.

I still have the scarf that Paula wrapped around my neck all those years ago. It reminds me that all things are possible, and in the joy of moving on and beginning again each day, knitting frees me to recover.

chapter nine

The Girl Who Cuts

PART OF MY REGULAR weekend routine includes snapping a leash on my yellow lab, Zena, and walking down a graveled path flanking a tree-lined creek behind my backyard. Rounding the corner, sunshine filters through the stand of trees keeping company with the bridge and takes the chill from my frosty fingers. The weather is perfect and I have time for a long, leisurely walk. A snowy egret shovels his neon feet under a pool of murky water, and the unmistakable squawk of a nearby night heron begins a glorious day. My camera catches a mother duck and her thirteen puffball, bumblebee-colored babies out for a morning lesson.

Occasionally, as my pooch is particularly pokey, I carry my knitting along to keep me occupied while she spends her own good time with her nose stuck in any one particular place. My knitting allows her time to sniff and keeps my impatience in check, so I don't choke her or yell at her to hurry up. I hate yanking on the poor girl.

A decision to walk in the same direction every morning pretty much ensures that we'll run into someone we know, and today is no exception. Behind me, a neighbor friend calls out. Jeanne catches up and, while our dogs meet and greet, she comments on how amazing it is that I can knit and walk at the same time.

"What are you working on?"

"Something mindless...a pair of socks." A ball of multicolored yarn peeks out from under my right armpit. Knitting, talking, and walking with two dogs is one thing too many, even for me, so I shove the sock and the self-striping yarn into my pocket. I like to pay attention when I walk with Jeanne and I listen to her every word because she's a therapist and I still think there might be something wrong with me.

"Yeah, right, mindless," she scoffs. "I don't know how you do it."

Over the course of time that our dogs have grown up and we've walked the path together, I've told her stories about my troubled years and bad behavior. She's seen the scars on my wrist and knows how they got there. Today, she notices a new tattoo that covers them, and, although she likes it, she wonders why anyone would choose to endure the pain of poking needles. I do my best to explain while both dogs pull us to the side of the path and push their snouts into the same bush.

"You know," she says, "yesterday at work in the counselor's office, I was told about a little girl...an eight-year-old in third grade who took a pencil and used the eraser to gouge a hole in her arm. She rubbed the eraser over and over in the same spot until it burned and then she kept gouging at herself until it bled."

My imagination grabs the pencil from Jeanne's words and presses it into my arm, scraping and gouging harder and harder, over and over until I can see the burn and feel the sting. I am a third grader trying to sit still at my desk with a yellow pencil, and then I am a sixth grader standing in my bathroom with a razor blade.

"Are you serious?" I ask, willing the vision away. "Are you kidding? They're using pencil erasers...in third grade?"

"I'm not kidding," Jeanne says. "Right now, self-harming is a real epidemic. It's in all the schools. Something like one in every two hundred girls between fourteen and nineteen cuts themselves on a regular basis. So many kids now, especially the younger ones, are cutting and burning themselves. Sometimes they scrape themselves with staples they carry around with them 'just in case,' and no one knows what to do about it."

"Oh my God, I had no idea." I feel sick and my mind races. What can I do, what can I do? I have to help them. I have to let them know that there are grown-ups who understand how they feel. I know how they feel. How can I reach them? The eight-year-old, I want to talk to her and tell her that I found a way to make the hurt stop.

"You know," Jeanne startles me from my mania. "You could help these kids...they would relate to you. You know how they feel. You know why they would want to cut themselves. You know about addiction and how you got better."

"I do...I can...but how? You work with the school counselors, aren't they talking to these kids?"

"The counselors are trying, but the kids aren't talking to them. We have to tell their parents and they freak out because they don't know what to do either. The kids need something; they need someone to talk to besides therapists and parents. You could reach them, I know it." We walk in silence with our own thoughts, the dogs sensing the end of the trail.

"You could teach them to knit. Look what it's done for you, look how far you've come. You could start a knitting therapy group. Hey, you could even start your own TV knitting therapy show...I'm serious." I laugh at the thought while rounding the corner toward home.

"Yeah, right, like anyone would want to watch a bunch of people knitting together and listen in on what they talk about." Well, actually, I would.

Tormented by the visual of the pencil and the knowledge that cutting is running rampant, I type "cutting statistics" into my web browser and, in that instant, my world is forever changed.

Finally, I have my answer. I know what it is that I'm supposed to do. I need to help them. I can tell them how I got fixed.

I can show them.

I smell Karen's coffee long before she arrives.

"What brings you to my lovely little office?" I ask, while she places a steaming mocha too close to the edge of my cluttered desk.

Karen and I met a few months ago at a business function and we struck up a conversation. Along with my knitting accomplishments, I don't know why, but as usual, I shared some of my tragic stories about overdoses, bad behavior, and alcohol-related mayhem. I hadn't heard from her for a while when she called and asked to see me.

"I have a friend starting up a nonprofit group for foster kids and she wants to know if you'll teach them how to knit." I nearly explode. This is the dream I've been waiting for. Of course I will.

"Foster kids? How old are they?"

"I think around eight or nine. I know there's a fourteen-year-old, too. My friend Shelly is starting this group for the kids to explore their creative talents through art, and we were thinking that knitting would be a perfect thing for them to learn. We have a meeting tomorrow morning and we want you to come. Are you interested?"

"Yes, yes, I'd love to!" I can hardly breathe.

"By the way," she says, turning to me before she's out the door. "One of the girls is a cutter."

The day has arrived. I'm supposed to meet Karen at Shelly's house where we'll pick up supplies for the kids. Anxiety keeps me panicked about getting lost or being late so constantly referring to paper directions gives me hope that I'll find my way. Rubbing my thumb and index finger together in a circular motion alleviates a bit of anxiety but, after a forty-five-minute drive and a lot of finger rubbing, I'm lost.

I want to go home, but I can't. I said I would be there. I volunteered so I have to go.

After several wrong turns, I find Shelly's house. Even though I know a second cup of coffee will give me a headache, I accept the offer while she and Karen gather supplies. Then we load her car with bins packed with donated yarn, picture frames, glue sticks, sparkles, and other things for the kids. I follow them to the teen center, nervous and excited but tired already, even after an extra dose of caffeine. Anxiety exhausts me.

The door to the facility is locked. Maybe I'll get to go home after all. Instead, we wait for a key. Sitting in the open doorway of my van filled with the smell of woolly sheep, I warm up in the morning sun and beg my head to stop hurting. I have no idea what to expect and the anticipation is killing me. This is what I said I want to do. I'm sure it is…I think it is. I need to teach the girl who cuts because I know I can help her.

At the same time the key arrives, a van pulls into the parking lot. Six or seven young children tumble out and a few scoot around in circles on little wheels under their shoes. I don't think I can do this. I don't know any of these people and the kids look too young to teach to knit. I don't see a teenager. I don't see the girl I came here to help.

"They're here!" Okay, I guess I'm not going home.

The center is a large rec room with several side rooms and an enormous front area with a curtained stage. I help Karen set out snack trays for the kids and then she points to the large classroom, brightly lit with overhead fluorescent lights and folding chairs around a group of four tables pushed together. I'm only expecting seven or eight, but it's nice to have a lot of room.

Unpacking and setting out needles like silverware at a party calms me a little, and the pile of colored yarn in the center of the table soothes my headache. The kids will love all these bright colors piled high in the center of the table. I feel a little better now, looking at the yarn.

"Okay, okay, kids, let's go, it's time for our very first knitting lesson." Shelly ushers them into the room.

I know I can do this. It just takes a little while to get started. I like to cast on and knit a few rows first because it just works better that way, a tried-and-true way for me to teach. The kids file in and I count past six to seven, then eight…nine…ten. I only brought needles for eight. Now what? Don't panic. I have a few more pairs in the box in the back of the van. I run to get them.

"How many of you have ever knit before?" I ask, hoping for at least a few raised hands. One nine-year-old says she tried to knit when she was younger but "didn't do very good." I keep a rolling conversation, asking questions about this and that while casting on twenty stitches and knitting two rows on ten needles. It takes too long and they get restless, so I hurry. A few of the kids are too young and I worry about losing my patience.

She's not here...the older girl, the cutter. I wonder where she is. I'm desperate to see her. She's the reason I came. I came to teach her, especially.

With all ten pairs finally cast on, I gravitate to the kids who've knit before. They usually get it pretty quickly, which means I can get to everyone before they start squirming. As soon as I have a child's attention and my hands wrapped around theirs, the knitting begins and the rest of the room disappears.

The minute she walks into the room, I know she's the one. They were right—Rachael looks much older than her fourteen years. She's definitely a pretty girl. I can't help but notice the lack of sheen in her home-dyed jet-black hair. Even though I know about her cutting and compulsive behavior, I try not to stare, but I want to see. I want to see where she hurts herself.

Her gold sparkly nail polish and silver lip piercing speaks volumes. She gives a quick smile when I look her way, and I feel her shyness in the way she sits down in the chair next to me on my left.

"I only have two balls of yarn left, what color would you like?" She points to the bright red.

"Okay, then, let's get you cast on and knitting." She seems somewhat at ease and eager to learn. With ten other children already having problems, questions, and some very large holes, I'm running circles around the table.

"A mistake doesn't matter, just keep going," I tell them. I really want to focus on Rachael. I cast on with her red yarn with one short, wooden bamboo needle, while she runs her fingers over the smoothness of the other.

Looking at her, it's not obvious she cuts herself or habitually pulls bits of hair from her scalp. While hot sauce was used as a thumb-sucking deterrent by my mother, it didn't prove effective in stopping me from biting my fingers. Remembering my own oblivion, I can understand how hair pulling wouldn't hurt. I want to let Rachael know that she's not alone.

I have twenty, bright red stitches on the needle and two rows knit. Considering her shyness, I take a gamble and lean in close as I hand her the sticks, close enough to smell the unmistakable scent of a recently smoked cigarette. It's not surprising to me that she smokes, and I'm sure she's already hit the drugs as well.

While she struggles to make her first stitch, I find myself staring at her teenage face, searching for the pain that lives just below the surface, searching for an answer. I want to know her. My own reflection looks back and I am appalled to see just how young I was when I first hurt myself.

"Here, let me show you." She doesn't speak while our hands touch. I guide them, wrapping each stitch with the working yarn and pulling a loop through, then off the end. "Put your fingers closer to the ends of the needles so you have more control. You have to use your fingers to hold the stitches so they don't slip off the tips of the needles."

Her shyness seems to lessen but still, she doesn't speak. She executes a few good-looking stitches so I make a quick circle around the tables to help the few remaining kids who need it. Several of the youngest have gone off to make something else in another room, which allows me to breathe easier and have fun with the remaining knitters.

After several successful rows, Rachael is doing a great job. Amazed at her progress and seeming at ease with the needles and yarn, she wraps stitch after stitch, properly and carefully without the usual grimace of a new knitter. I forget about the holes in her scalp or the scars I can't see on her arms and wrists.

"Look at you, you're a knitter! Look how perfect your stitches are. Are you sure you've never knit before?"

"No, I never have," she almost laughs. "It's fun, though, I like it."

Our eyes connect for the first time.

"How bad did it hurt to have your lip pierced?" I ask. "I'm too old for one, but I like it, it's totally cool."

"It hurt pretty bad, but not as bad as this one." She pulls her hair back a tiny bit to show me the piercing in the cartilage at the top of her ear. I'm surprised at the gesture and unable to see very well. I slowly and purposefully reach toward her face and, gently, with the back of my hand, sweep her hair back to get a better look at the earring. She doesn't flinch. My heart races; she let me touch her hair. I'm sure she doesn't let just anybody touch her hair.

"Whoa, that's totally cool."

"Thanks."

I want to tell her what happened to me and how I got better, how making these stitches one after another, day after day, helped me feel better about myself. Too soon, it's time to go and, of course, now that I'm here, I want to stay.

"Okay, gang, keep practicing because the more you do it, the better you get, and don't worry if you mess up, just keep going. I'll be back, so we can keep knitting, okay?" Rachael shakes her head yes.

On the way out, I think about the whole adventure and how it was a success in so many ways. I got out of the house, didn't panic when I got lost, and managed to teach a bunch of kids to knit. On the drive home, it occurs to me that I never once saw her tug at her hair. Not once...the whole time she was knitting.

I can't wait to see her again, but it doesn't happen. The group moves on to other activities. Disappointment doesn't come close to how I feel. This was the one girl I wanted to reach. I was hoping we would knit and talk, but we never got the chance.

It's been months and I think about Rachael a lot. I wonder if she's still cutting and pulling her hair out. I wonder if she's knitting; knitting might have been able to make a difference.

Karen came to my office today. She brought me something. She handed me a photograph of a teenager wearing a red beret, a smile, and a long red scarf, obviously hand knit. The jet-black hair hanging from under the hat has a sheen like I've never seen.

part four
Mending

chapter ten

Lost but Not Forgotten

I MET NINETEEN-YEAR-OLD Tanya at a residential foster group home where I was invited to attend one of their weekly mandatory meetings to try to generate interest in a free knitting group. What better place to teach knitting than a home for emancipated foster youth? I didn't know about emancipation before I read an article; I didn't know that on the day you turn eighteen, your foster parents are no longer responsible and some of them toss you out on the street. These kids would be homeless if it wasn't for this facility. I didn't know that kids could be homeless.

Although it's nighttime and the road is dimly lit, I'm not worried about getting lost because the neighborhood is familiar.

With no artwork on ghastly green walls and narrow halls, I feel like I'm in an institution, but there's no time to linger on the memory of the locked ward where I spent a three-week nightmare.

Single-room doors line both sides of the hallway as far as I can see. A whiff brings a faint odor and now I remember that this was a convalescent hospital and an eeriness creeps up my spine.

After I ask a few teens for directions, I locate the living room area and sit in a plastic chair in the back corner. Already, a half a dozen youth are plopped on two leather couches while the rest of the residents sit in chairs or stand along the front wall.

The counselor in charge starts the meeting and addresses the usual problems that twenty-year-olds have—where not to smoke, how to empty a garbage can, and how to turn the volume down on a boom box. I shake my head, agreeing to follow the rules, as if I belong to the group and live here because I want them to notice me and I need them to accept me. I have to find out if knitting can help them.

The counselor, not remembering my name, introduces me as a person with an announcement, and then I stand up and sweat.

Desperate to connect, I tug at the sleeves of my sweater to expose my tattoos, so they won't think of me as some "old lady" knitter. After addressing the group with my plans to "hang out and teach anybody who wants to learn to knit," five or six seem interested. I'm ecstatic. I have a group of at-risk kids to teach and piles of donated yarn and needles. I sit down and I'm so excited that I don't hear the rest of the rules.

When the meeting adjourns, a tall dark-haired girl with black lipstick approaches.

"I saw your tattoo from across the room. It's totally cool." I stick my arm out for her to get a better look and tell her how the vines and roses cover a bunch of old cutting scars. She acknowledges the scars, as if they're nothing out of the ordinary and I'm not surprised, because her appearance makes me believe that she might be part of the group that knows about scars and cutting.

"I can't come tomorrow because I have school."

"No worries, maybe another time." A shorter girl with slicked-back hair in a ponytail walks over, and the tall girl walks away.

"I heard you say you have scars. How did you stop? I still cut myself and I want to stop. I'm pregnant and I don't want to do it anymore. How did you do it?"

Her question catches me off guard and unprepared, but I have to tell her something and all that I can think of in that second is how knitting pretty much saved my life, so I tell her that.

"It wouldn't hurt for you to give it a try." She rolls her eyes. "Will you come tomorrow?" I ask.

"Yeah, I'll come."

In the light of day, the living room is larger than it seemed, housing a full-sized pool table, a dining table for eight, and the two leather couches. Double French doors at the side open to a sunny patio, and an open doorway on the other side leads to a large industrial kitchen. I bring two large boxes filled with donated yarn and fifteen pairs of needles. I park myself at the dining room table and take out my knitting.

It's three o'clock and a few teens arrive. I have to coax them in, but in a short time, there are six—four girls and two guys. Surprisingly, two of the girls and one of the guys already know how to knit and the other two girls crochet. The other boy wants to sew patches on his denim jacket. Next week I'll have to remember to bring a needle and thread.

They rifle through the boxes of yarn. Everyone wants to know if they can have more than one ball, then they toss them around like footballs before settling down at the table. Adolescent chatter flies as crochet hooks chain chains and needles remember how to make stitches. This is going to be great. I just have to show up and let them talk. And talk, they do.

"So, are all of you living here because when you turned eighteen, you didn't have a place to go?" The thought of this sickens me, kids left to fend for themselves at eighteen, especially foster kids. I can't imagine what that would feel like.

They all nod, and then one of the girls asks me, "You wanna know what I did to get back at my foster mother?" No one looks up from their works in progress.

"What?" I ask her, because I do want to know. This is exactly why I want them to knit, so they can manage their anxiety and whatever else they might be going through.

"The day I turned eighteen, the bitch took every single thing I owned and threw it out into the street. Everything. On my birthday. But I got her good. You wanna know what I did?" She throws her head back and smiles. "I burned that house down. To the ground." My jaw drops.

"You got busted for that, then?" I ask, after an awkward silence.

"Nope." She seems so proud. "Nobody ever found out it was me."

I'm shocked. Not so much at what she did—I know the kind of pain that would allow a person to start a fire—but I'm more blown away by her arrogance and decision to share her arson with a complete stranger. No one else bats an eye. I wonder if this is for real so I decide not to inquire further as this goes beyond even my expertise. She's got her crochet chain going, though, and that's what I decide to concentrate on.

The girl to her left, Tanya, is crocheting a long chain as well. Just as I'm about to comment on what a great job she's doing, she flings it across the table.

"I wanna learn how to knit, instead."

"Okay, do you want a different yarn?"

"No, duh."

Just as I get up to help her get started, she smacks the table with the palms of both hands.

"Nope, never mind, I'll just do this." She snatches a few balls and cuts a piece of yarn from each one and then ties them to the back of her chair. When I give her the what-are-you-talking-about look, she tells me that she's going to make a braid.

For a minute she stays focused, and then she tells me that she wants to make a blanket for her baby "'cause I'm prego." She wants "rainbow yarn, not light, you know, bright colors all in one ball, like a rainbow." Now I recognize her from the night before. Her hair is down...she's the one who asked me how I stopped cutting. I'll be buying some rainbow yarn.

The next week on a sunny afternoon, I arrive with another box of yarn. Sitting on the bench at the front entrance, Tanya looks up from the paper she's writing, tips her head sideways, and gives me a smirk.

"Doing homework?" I ask.

"No duh, what's wrong with you? Why would you even ask me a stupid question like that? I'll be inside in a minute."

"I have something for you, something special, just for you," I call back. She's a pain, but no one can give me anything I haven't dished out myself many times before.

"The rest can't come today," Tanya mumbles on the way in.

I must have looked confused. "What?" she asks. She stares at me like I'm an idiot.

"Do you want to hang out on the couch then, or sit at the table?" Her purple boom box will ensure a music montage during our crochet lesson and I hope she isn't into rap. I hand her three skeins of rainbow yarn.

"Good for a boy or girl," she says, and sits down on the worn sofa. She grabs a skein of yarn, looks it over, and promptly throws it back into my lap.

"How do you open this stupid thing?"

I show her how to find the end in the middle and toss it back just as hard. She makes a slipknot and starts hooking a very long chain.

"That's probably long enough," I warn. "That much chain will make a blanket big enough to fit a king size bed, and you only have three skeins." She rips out a few feet of chain and looks for approval.

"Perfect." I nod.

While she stitches into her chain, I crochet a baby hat. My first attempt is too big for a newborn, but Tanya likes it so I start another. I really want to break through her toughness and know more about her. Will crocheting help her relax, like knitting does for me? It's a long road, but I'm hoping she'll find a way to stop cutting.

"There was a huge fight here last night," she breaks our silence. "The cops had to come and everything. It was a mess, but I don't care. I'm leaving soon anyway."

"What? Why are you leaving?" Shoot, I just got this girl to start to open up. I want to stay connected to her.

"You can't have babies here."

"Where will you go?"

"To live with my real mother. She's been out of rehab for nine months."

"How does your mom feel about the baby, is she excited?" No response. Before I realize that I have gone into forbidden territory, I stupidly ask if she's excited about the baby. She continues crocheting without a word. Oops, I've gone too far.

She finishes a couple of rows by the time I crochet two baby hats. Something finally dawns on her. "You bought this for me?"

"Well, you said you needed rainbow yarn." She murmurs a thank you and then offers me some of her food.

"Do you want to read my poem?" As soon as I say yes, a folded yellow paper catapults across the dirty glass coffee table.

ME
Dazed and Confused,
Lost and Abused,
Pain and Sorrow,
Maybe no tomorrow.
Pushed Away,
to rot and decay,
tossed and turned,
toasted and burned.
Faded and Dark,
A hurtful remark,
A stab in the back,
Just another crack.
Broken and Done,
okay, you won,
No more strain,
No more pain.

"Look, I have three rows done!" Tanya says.

"It's perfect." I look up, reeling from the words on the paper, which are so similar to the kind of words I wrote so many years ago.

A few weeks later, Tanya calls me and asks for a ride. She wants to meet her mother after church later in the day. I'm teaching another group of younger foster kids to knit and I ask her if she'd like to go with me.

"If you can drop me off at church after, I guess I'll go."

"Bring your crochet," I tell her. When I pick her up, I'm happy to see that she has it with her. As long as we're spending time together, I ask her some questions.

"When you were cutting yourself, did you really want to die?" She slumps into the passenger seat.

"After so much...I just had enough."

"What happened to you?"

She rattles off six or seven states she'd been moved around to, how much time she's spent in juvenile hall and institutions, and then she tells me that she jumped off of a three-story building and put herself in a coma for four days, and then that she sliced the top of her head open with a razor blade.

"I spent a lot of time in an institution for that one!" She laughs. I can't believe what I'm hearing. No wonder she's a mess.

"Are you serious? Why would you do that? Were you drinking?"

"I never drink or do drugs." She is adamant. "My foster mother—my adopted mother—beat the crap out of me...yeah, from the time I was three until I was eleven."

She looks out the side window and shrugs her shoulders a few times. She doesn't say another word. I drop her at church and I'm exhausted.

Three months later, I get an urgent call from Tanya.

She asks if I would buy her some diapers and bring some pink yarn because she lost her blanket and crochet hook when she moved from her motel after she had the baby.

"Will you bring some extra?" she asks. "I want to teach my mom how to crochet. She'll be a year sober tomorrow and she really wants to learn how."

Of course I will.

I bring her diapers. She lost custody temporarily, but sees her daughter once a week at her new job where she works in exchange for rent. Even if you don't ask, she'll show you a phone full of pictures, as proud as any mother could be.

"Still crocheting?" I have to know.

"No, duh," she smiles.

chapter eleven

A Way Out

AT SIXTEEN, MARY HAS taken all the abuse from her father that she can stand. Finally, she takes her babysitting money and her belongings and walks out the front door. With her money running out, she has to do something, so she puts on a dress and applies for a waitress job at a diner.

Two weeks later on a Sunday afternoon, a motorcycle roars into the parking lot. Heads turn when he walks in, especially Mary's. He's the handsomest boy she's ever seen and she can't take her eyes off of him. His name is Victor, but he says she can call him Vic.

When her shift is over they roar out of the parking lot together. With her arms wrapped around his leather jacket and the wind in her face, she feels safe and happy for the first time in her life.

They ride to his grandmother's house, where he said he has his own apartment in the basement. Mary thought he would take her there, but he brings her upstairs to the front door instead.

"I want you to meet her," he says. "You can call her Nana, too." He unlocks the front door and as Mary follows him in, he calls to his grandmother.

"Come in, come in, Victor. How was your lunch?" A tea-colored tablecloth in the hallway catches Mary's eye and Nana notices her staring at it. "Oh, hello dear, come in, it's lovely, isn't it? That's my very first pineapple doily."

"Yes, I...I've never seen one, it's beautiful." Mary smiles at his grandma, hunched over and with a few teeth missing. But the way her eyes twinkle makes Mary feel good.

"You should see the rest of the house, then," Victor says, and he introduces Mary to Nana. She cups both of her hands and jiggles then up and down, shaking them for what seems like a very long time. Nana's hands are soft and warm.

"So nice to meet you, Miss Mary." She pats her in the small of her back. "Now, would you like to see what else I've made? Victor, get Mary something to drink, would you dear?" She winks at Victor and Mary feels like she might be dreaming.

"I'd love to see what you've made," Mary says shyly.

"I'll see you in a week, then." Victor laughs as he hugs his Nana and walks past Mary into the kitchen.

The musty rooms are filled with furniture as old as she must be. Nana leads Mary by the hand through each room. Cream-colored doilies cover the arms and backs of every chair, and knickknacks sit on them on every table. There must be hundreds. In her room, a calico cat sleeps nestled in a white doily that covers the bed and hangs to the floor.

"You made all of these?" Mary asks. "I've never seen anything like it!"

"Why, yes, of course," Nana smiles. "Don't you crochet?"

"No, I've heard of it, but I've never seen anything as beautiful as these." Nana hands Mary a doily. "It looks like lace and I love lacy things."

"Well, then, Mary, I'll just have to teach you how to crochet." Vic comes back with two cups of hot tea and Mary hands the doily back to Nana.

"I'd love to learn how to make these someday."

"Nana," he says, "Mary has nowhere to go, and I want to invite her to stay with me, if that's okay."

This is the first Mary is hearing of this, but she's head-over-heels and it sounds like a great plan to her. Wow, a boyfriend, a grandma, and a place to stay all in one day. Can her life get any better?

"Of course she can stay, dear." Nana sits down and tells Mary how her grandmother taught her to crochet. Mary loves her already.

Over the next few months, Vic and Mary spend their days at work and evenings with Nana. Vic sits in Nana's chair and watches while the two of them sit on the couch together. Nana teaches Mary how to use a tiny steel hook and fine cotton thread and after a few sloppy starts, she has a little circle going and it looks like it might become lace after all. She makes a mistake and has to rip it out and start over and then Nana tells her not to fret over mistakes, because everybody makes mistakes.

On their days off, Vic and Mary ride the motorcycle everywhere, wrapped in love and each other. One day, Vic asks her to marry him and she is the happiest girl in the world.

That night, during teatime, they plan to tell Nana of their engagement. When they get upstairs, Nana is in the kitchen fretting because she is out of tea.

"Be a dear and run off to the store now, will you, Victor?" While Mary sits down for another crochet lesson, she hears Vic rev up his engine.

"I know he's happy, because whenever he thinks about me, he revs up the engine," Mary smiles at Nana. "It's our special happy thing."

Nana grins a wrinkled smile back.

A mile down the road, a speeding car races through a red light at an intersection and careens into a motorcycle, hitting the bike from behind, tossing the rider like a rag-doll through the air until he smashes into the pavement fifty feet in front of the bike.

Vic stays in a coma for twelve days. When he wakes up, he has no memory of Mary, of Nana, or of anything else. His family comes to take care of him, family he never talked about, and Mary has to leave because "we don't want you here," they say. And by the way, they'll be moving Nana to a senior home.

Before Mary leaves, Nana gives her a kiss, three steel hooks, and a cone of cotton.

Mary, stunned, knows that she wants to keep her job, but it's too much to think about so she packs her backpack, cashes her paycheck, and walks to the bus station. When the man behind the counter asks her where she's going, she tells him that she doesn't know—"No, I really don't know,"—so she steps out of line and takes a seat in the corner next to a girl who looks as sad as she feels. Nana's cotton cone pokes her in the back and she drops her face into her hands and bawls like a baby.

Mary buys a ticket to Tacoma. Her head hurts and the only thing she can think of is Nana and Vic, and how messed up her life is, and how could this happen, and she wants to die. There are only a few people on the bus, so she takes a seat to herself. She wants to sleep, but every time she closes her eyes, all she sees is Vic and Nana, and she sees the look in Nana's eyes when Nana kissed her goodbye.

The bus pulls into a parking lot and more people get on. A girl has a bandage over her left eye and the sight of it causes Mary to drift back to Mrs. Peterson's fourth grade class. Janet Newberry is calling her "Franken-face" because of the fluorescent green stitches that she got over her eye after her father bashed her head into the closet door. Mrs. Peterson is writing something on the chalkboard and Janet says it again, louder this time, in case someone didn't pay attention, and then all the kids call Mary "Franken-face" for two weeks.

The girl with the bandage sits in the seat a couple rows in front of her and Mary watches while she takes a ball of yarn the color of sky from her bag, and then she cannot see what else because her vision is blurred. She feels Nana's warm hands guiding hers while they sit and crochet together and Mary opens her bag and there is Nana, all wrapped up in the cone, and she finds her hook and makes a few stitches. The comfort that washes over her is almost too much to bear.

When Mary gets off the bus, she falls in love, gets pregnant, and gets married. She's in love for such a short time that she finds out, too late, what a mistake she made. Usually, it's just a lot of shoving, but sometimes he hits her hard and takes her keys and then he blocks the door when she tries to get out.

Their daughter is nine months old and Mary is pregnant again and she's elated when the doctor puts her on total bed rest. Her husband dotes on his precious baby girl, and his anger won't reach Mary if she's quiet and stays in her place. For the next few months, he is calm and life is calm.

A person can only stay in bed so long before they start to go bonkers. Mary's used and reused Nana's cotton so many times that the cone looks like it's wrapped in ramen noodles. She wants to make something for her daughter, but she doesn't know how to get help. She keeps trying to remember what Nana taught her, but she messes it up every time.

On the rare occasion that her husband is away, Mary takes his computer and climbs back into bed and her world opens to a place she never knew existed. She finds people online...and videos online...and crocheters online. Mostly, she's glued to the crochet videos and she practices and practices. She finds a community on Facebook and makes friends, and as her crochet skills grow, so does her confidence.

It takes weeks to make anything come out the way it's supposed to, but then she really gets the hang of it. It's all so exciting. She makes dishcloths with lace edges and round doilies. Despite the fact that she hears nothing but negativity and how everything she makes looks horrid, she can't put the hook down.

She finds a pattern for a lace bonnet and decides to make two. Mary begins to get offers, and requests for her work, and is actually able to make money...her own money. With Nana's remaining cotton, she crochets a christening gown and sells it for what seems like a fortune.

With every crochet stitch that she makes, Nana's warmth and love flows through her fingers. With her newfound self-esteem, she finds the strength to pack up and leave.

I met Mary through Facebook and asked her to share her story with me.

"When I crochet, the rest of the world floats away and my brain goes somewhere nice and I hear a soothing voice. I hear Nana's voice and she is sitting next to me, helping me sort myself out," she wrote me.

"I have a new apartment now, two beautiful daughters, and a bucket full of crochet hooks. My designs bring in money to help support me and the girls, and just when I think things can't get any better, I get a job teaching crochet at a yarn shop close enough to walk to. The girls get so excited when they get to help me pick out colors for a project, and with any leftover yarn, I crochet hats for a local women's shelter. I never imagined a life filled with so much joy. When people ask who taught me how to crochet, the words fall right out of my heart.

"My Nana did."

chapter twelve

A Million Miles Away

"MY GRANDMOTHER DID," Abbey says, when I ask who taught her how to knit. "She knit with thick, gray, lanolin wool that stunk like sheep. She was always picking out little bits of sticks and hay."

A few affirmative nods bob around the table and a lanolin discussion ensues—whether it's good to leave it in, as it makes for soft hands, or better not to have yarn that smells like a barnyard. Personally, I love the smell. Abbey is the newest member of our regular Tuesday knitting group, which brings tonight's attendance to six. She focuses on her raspberry lace shawl, but continues her story.

"The only thing I ever saw her make were mittens and wool socks. We went through lots of socks because Wisconsin winters were freezing. She knit them much bigger than they were supposed to be and then she boiled and felted them so they were toasty warm. Whenever we got the chance to visit her on the farm, she made room for me next to her in the rocking chair. The whole time she knit, she would tell me stories about our family, like she was reading from an invisible book."

Nostalgia brings my grandmother, cross-stitching in her rocking chair, with the sun from the front window dozing in her lap and songs from her caged canaries echoing through the house. I remember her farmyard in Connecticut where my brother and I teased the giant buffalo behind the wobbly fence.

"One day, I took a little piece of that gray wool and wound it around and around my finger while I listened to her voice. I fidgeted with the yarn for a few minutes and then I asked her if she would teach me to knit."

"How old were you?" Anne looks up from her cream-colored baby booties.

"I think I was only six, but I remember the day perfectly. It was summertime. Grandma kept the front and back kitchen doors open—not a good idea on a dairy farm, but she covered the doorways with mosquito netting to keep flies out. We sat in her rocking chair together and I remember a warm breeze blowing. Grandma smelled like fresh-cut hay drying in the fields. Warm, like cows in the barn. She smelled like dirt and vegetables and chicken eggs."

Abbey drops a stitch and hands it to me so I can fix it. At the other end of the table someone mentions bacon and now I smell bacon sizzling and it feels like a Sunday morning.

"So finish your story. Tell us more about your grandma," Marcie pipes in.

"Well, when I asked her to teach me to knit, she looked at me over her glasses, like she always did, and without a word, went to her basket and brought out a wooden spool, a tiny crochet hook, and a ball of mixed-up colored yarn that I'd never seen before. I wasn't sure what the spool was for because I was expecting knitting needles, but I was excited anyway. She showed me how to pull the yarn through the center of the spool with the crochet hook, and then wind it around each of four small finishing nails that she said Grandpa had hammered in around the hole."

Abbey demonstrates the motion to the group on an imaginary spool. "I caught on pretty quick, I loved the colors. Blue came out first, then red, green, and yellow. Each time I gave the end of the cord a tug, a millimeter would appear, and another color would peek out. Grandma said I could use the cord to make a carpet, or use it to hold my mittens together, or I could make ties for my winter hat or clothes for my doll. Every time I think about it, it reminds me how much that first cord was the beginning of my love for knitting."

Several knitters share their spool stories; I think we all had them. I tell the group how my father made a bunch for my brother and me, and we made miles and miles of the colorful cording. After playing with it (my Ginny doll had the best carpet in her cardboard house), we wound it into a ball the size of a watermelon.

"Is your grandma still around?"

"No," she sighs. "After a few years, her stories broke off and became fewer, as if her life had suddenly crashed. Most of the stories she told after that were only about relatives and she didn't include herself. It took me a long time to find out why."

"What happened?" I can't help asking. In unison, the group stops knitting and looks in her direction.

Abbey doesn't miss a stitch. "Knitting takes my brain to somewhere nice, you know? When I knit, my grandmother is there, sitting next to me, talking, and helping me figure things out. I fidget a lot, but if I'm crocheting or knitting, all of that goes away. My mind slows down. I get into a rhythm and the world falls away. Nothing else matters. I'm a million miles away just floating along." She obviously doesn't want to talk about what happened.

I reach over and lightly massage Abbey's back for a second. I want her to know that I know the place too, where you get to float away and, no matter what bad things happen, you can find a place where no hurt lives.

It's time to go. Knitting group is over and the store is closing. Abbey's demeanor changes to lighthearted and she apologizes to the girls for her ramble.

"You don't think we come here just to knit, do you?" Mary winks.

The girls stuff their knitting accoutrements into bags and boxes and after hugs all around, head for the exit. I notice Abbey's knitting still on the table.

"I have a key, we can stay if you want," I say. Maybe she'll tell me what happened to her grandmother.

"Really? I would love to stay and knit. I'm home alone for a few days."

Our water cooler has instant boiling water, so I ask if she wants a cup of tea. As I make us one, she asks how long we can stay.

"Until the cows come home." I laugh at my stupid comment and we bring our tea to the table. We start knitting in the quiet and after a few minutes, I ask what happened to her grandmother.

"It's a long story. She was abused. What happened to her is same thing that my father did to me."

Shoot. Now I don't want to know and I wish I'd kept my mouth shut. I don't like father stories, but I can't think about mine right now because Abbey is already talking.

"I guess I was dyslexic. My father thought I wasn't

able to keep numbers and things in the right order on purpose, and he would hit me and tell me how stupid I was every time I was wrong. Sometimes, I can still hear him laughing and calling me names."

My father didn't hit me, but the stupid part we have in common.

"He always made empty promises. If you do this, you can have this. The problem was, when I did receive something good, like a bottle of soda, as soon as it was open, he would ask for a sip and drink the whole thing."

"Oh my God, he sounds just like my father. All of us kids played chess, and he told us that if any of us could beat him, he would give us twenty dollars. Back then, that was a ton of money. I practiced with my brother and sister as much as they would play with me. I played almost every day, and one day, the big day came. I beat him. I was so proud of myself that I could hardly stop jumping up and down. After a look of disgust, he got up. When he returned, I just stared at what he handed me because I couldn't believe my eyes. I worked so hard to prove to him that I could be a winner and what did he give me? A twenty dollar bill from the stupid Monopoly game."

I realize I'm yelling, still humiliated, as if it happened yesterday.

"That must have hurt."

My knitting is tight, something that never happens, and I can't get the stitches to move so I tear out the row and put it down. "I was devastated, and really mad. Guess I still am."

"My father used mental torture that he thought highly hilarious as well," says Abbey. "Most likely, because it was at my expense. I was too stupid to catch on until I'd look up from what I was doing, or walk into the room and find him rolling with laughter, like I was the idiot."

"What a jackass."

"When I was seven or eight, all I ever wanted was a pet fish, but every time I asked, the answer was always no because the cats would eat it, he said." I pick up my knitting and she puts hers down. It's really hard to work on lace and talk at the same time.

"I came home from school and my father, sitting at his customary place at the head of the table, looks at me with that jerky smile...I should have known...and then he tells me he has a surprise for me in the barn, in a bucket in the milk house. He says he found something that I really, really want and if I hurry, it'll be mine. I thought he finally got me a goldfish and I ran so fast that my heels were slapping my bottom all the way across the yard. When I yanked the barn door open and pushed through the milk house door, the stainless steel bucket was exactly where he said it would be.

"It had a few inches of water in it, but nothing else. No fish, nothing. I burst out crying and screaming at the barn cats for eating my goldfish. I wanted to kill them."

"The cats ate the fish?"

"Wait...so I'm sobbing my heart out, walking back to the house. About halfway across the yard, I hear laughter—loud, raucous laughter. I'm still crying on my way into the kitchen and my dad is almost falling off his chair. My mother's just sitting there, looking sort of sad and resigned. My father asks me what's wrong, so I tell him the cats ate my goldfish. He's still laughing hysterically and then he yells 'April fools.'"

What a rotten thing to do to a kid. If she wasn't so

upset, I might laugh at the scenario, at least her father had a sense of humor. I keep my mouth shut.

"I never forgave him for that. I thought the cats ate my fish, the only thing I ever wanted, and he thought it was so funny. Then I spent years worrying that something was really wrong with me because I actually thought about killing the cats to teach them a lesson."

My recurring nightmare of choking cats to death pushes its way to the front of my mind. I feel their razor-sharp teeth embed into my wrist and, as quick as it comes, with the next few stitches, the vision disappears. Her story, although a bit humorous, is bringing up a lot of crap.

Abbey picks up her lacework and makes a yarn over and a knit two together.

Her voice softens, as though she's young again. "I used to wet the bed every night. My father would beat me, tease me, and punish me in all sorts of ways. He would shame me in front of other people with comments about urine smells, stains, or just sniff me as I walked by and pinch his nose. I can't count the nights I slept in the bathtub because I couldn't find new sheets to change my bed, freezing my butt off with a towel under me and one on top to keep me warm. The woodstove in our drafty old farmhouse usually went out around four o'clock in the morning.

"Once, while I was at school, he hung the sheet I wet from the night before outside my window; the one I'd stuffed deep in the clothes hamper that morning. He thought that if my school chums knew that I wet the bed then I'd stop. Of course, they all saw it when the bus let me off. After that, I was the whipping kid. Even the teachers turned a blind eye. I was teased, beaten, buried in snow, and had hockey pucks slap-shot at me during recess. So my school years were miserable. My father made me the most unpopular kid in school."

"My God, Abbey, I thought my childhood was bad."

"I was always sick, but no one would take me to the doctor's for fear of them finding bruises from my father's boots or belt or shaving strap. I remember him dragging me out from the back of a closet where I was hiding. He'd pull me out and have me stand in front of him and show him all my bruises so he could apply a layer of Vaseline. It was supposed to make them go away faster he said. I don't know if it ever did, but I never wore short sleeves or went without tights to school, even on the hottest days. Most of my tights were ripped at the knees because I fell down a lot. It didn't help that I couldn't see where I was going, so the final insult was a thick pair of black plastic horn-rimmed glasses."

I have to physically close my gaping jaw with the heel of my hand.

"So there you have it, a skinny, sickly kid with long scraggly dirty auburn hair, scabby knees, bruises everywhere, thick black glasses hanging off the end of my nose, and always expecting a kick or a punch from passing kids. Not a pretty picture. I hate it even now, after all these years. I hate that girl."

This is hard for me. I know what it feels like to hate that girl.

"I used to never want to talk about it, but over the years I've found that the more I do, the more I learn about me, about how to cope with the mess that is my life, there are times when I have no answers and can't find any. I've come to that crossroad again, the one that has no signposts and I don't know what to do. I want to take the right path for once. I want to stop feeling sad deep inside, I want to feel happy, I want to be able to trust someone's promise, I want to find the solution that will stop me from sabotaging myself because I'm tired of failure, of feeling like a failure, like I'll never do anything right with my life. I'm fifty years old and I have little to show for myself."

"What about that beautiful shawl that's growing from your hands?" I say. I know it doesn't come close to what she needs to hear, but I'm so caught up, it's all I've got. "I'm sorry, Abbey. We've been through a lot of the same hurt. Every day that I knit, though, a little more of the pain that lives in the back of my head goes away. Knitting is my success. Everything I've accomplished tells me that my father was wrong."

Abbey's eyes glaze over and she reaches for a tissue.

"My father beat the crap out of me, and the way it usually goes, so did my first husband. While I was caught in his cycle of abuse, I sewed clothes for my kids; it was a way out of the nightmare for a few hours at a time. My son was disabled and things got so bad that I thought about suicide a lot...how I'd do it, where, when. Every scenario involved taking my son with me, since I knew no one knew how to take care of him properly. Or at least that's what I kept telling myself. I don't know if I really wanted to die, but I would take too many pain-killers, too many valiums, alcohol...anything I could get my hands on. It makes me sick now to think that I even had thoughts about taking my son with me. Thank God for knitting."

"Yeah, thank God for knitting." I stand up and start collecting my stuff. My head hurts. "Let's get out of here, I'm whooped."

While driving home, I think about Abbey's grand-mother and how the nuns beat her because she was left-handed, about how Abbey's father teased her, and how much we have in common, especially how knitting allows us to float away and make the rest of the world disappear. I wonder what horrible thing could have happened to her grandmother, and by the time I get home I'm trying to forget about that fake twenty-dollar bill.

It's late and I'm exhausted, but perfectly knitted stitches drop from my needles. My mind slows down. I get into a rhythm and the world falls away. Nothing else matters. I'm a million miles away, just floating along. Thank God for knitting.

chapter thirteen

Street Teens

THE ONLY TIME I don't enjoy the three boxes full of brightly colored yarn in the backseat of my car is on shopping day, because I have to figure out how to load the week's groceries. My car is full of yarn and needles.

"At least you have a car...and food," Nancy responds to my complaint.

"And I'm thankful for that." I give her a gentle shove as our knitting foursome walks down the sidewalk to the ice cream shop.

Back at the yarn store, Kathy struggles to find a way to embroider a dragonfly onto the center panel of her afghan while her mint chocolate chip melts in the cup. My pink plastic spoon takes a nosedive into the chocolate sprinkles and digs into the fudge at the bottom of my sundae.

"Mmmm, chocolate." Before I get the first spoonful down, though, it loses its power to satisfy because, after Nancy's comment, I'm thinking about the man with the cardboard sign that I drove past on the way here. Whenever I see a person holding a sign, I don't fully understand how it is that they let themselves get homeless.

Just get a job, I think, each time I pass one. How hard is that?

When I would see a homeless person in the winter, though, bundled in mismatched layers against the cold, I would wonder what he might think if I stopped and gave him a hand-knit blanket if I had one with me. As I would drive by, I would imagine him warm in his cardboard box in the woods next to the creek, and how grateful he would be to the stranger who thought about him and stopped to give him something for comfort. On the other hand, he might not appreciate it. He probably would rather have a drink. Besides, I couldn't imagine giving up one of my afghans to someone I didn't know. I think about it, especially when the weather turns cold, but I never put a blanket in my car.

Kathy needs some direction with her project and the three of us offer opinions and advice until finally she decides to embroider a black border with a backstitch around her paper pattern. After a few minutes, she holds it up for us to see.

"Perfect," I tell her. "It's going to look just like a dragonfly."

I'm still thinking about the homeless man and the seven hundred homeless kids that will be sleeping on the streets in my city tonight, and then I finish my ice cream.

"Nancy?"

"Yes, dear?" She draws out the "dear."

"Didn't you say that you worked with homeless kids when you were young...a long, long...long time ago?"

Her cone now consumed, she exaggerates the licking of each finger and then bonks me with her elbow.

"I did."

"Whatever happened with that?" Napkins tossed into a wastebasket, we settle into knitting.

"Well, I was pretty young. I was fifteen when I ran off after being homeschooled. I couldn't get a 'real' job, so I spent the next few years serving food in a soup kitchen, and then I babysat kids at church. That's where I met my husband. He was in college and working at a residential treatment center...I didn't even know what that was. He visited kids in jail and detention centers. I'd make brownies for them and some Christmas stuff but I never really got involved. Then we moved to Arcata."

"Hey, that's where one of my twins goes to college," I interrupt. "In fact, this beanie hat is for one of the guys on the rowing crew...only six more to go. Not sure if these are exactly the perfect college colors, but they're close enough. I love that four-hour drive north." Kathy puts her dragonfly away and pulls out a purple scarf. Nancy brings me back from a mental visit with my daughter with a playful tap of her needle on the table.

Nancy continues. "When we got to Arcata, I heard that they needed youth workers at one of the local churches so my husband and I started volunteering with a bunch of redneck druggie kids. I was totally out of my element."

Elisabeth looks up from her knitting. "You know what they say about Arcata, then?"

"I do now," Nancy says. "It didn't take long for us to find out that we were living in the emerald triangle, where all the pot grows, and that, in this little mountain town, these kids were second- and third-generation druggies. Some of them told us they got their first hit as toddlers from their parents in the form of 'special butter' and 'special brownies.'

"We tried to do fun things, but it was obvious that these kids couldn't even play team sports, they barely knew how to take care of themselves. We would see them eating ramen noodles out of the bag on the way to hang out with us at the church. I couldn't stand knowing they were hungry, so it wasn't long before my husband and I invited them to our house for dinner. We didn't have much to offer, but I could stretch a chicken. It was heartbreaking when they left the house because we knew that some of them were sleeping on the trails in the woods at night."

No one takes another stitch.

"It was around that time that I got seriously hooked on knitting. We took the kids to concerts on the square, trips, and campouts. Some had never even seen the ocean. I knit everywhere we went. They took great interest and finally asked if I would teach them.

"It wasn't long before I had a circle of girls knitting and let me tell you something, these weren't cheerleaders, either. These girls had tattoos and chains, and they had to hand over their knives at the front door. They learned how to make squares and we made blankets. Then they wanted to make fingerless gloves. Eventually, we made little felted purses with skulls on them. One day, one of the guys playing football decided that he wanted to learn how to knit. That was one of the best days ever. We were surprised when a few other boys joined the circle.

"I took the kids and their knitting everywhere. We knit in the emergency room when one of the kids' mothers was coming off a drug binge. We knit baby booties for pregnant teen moms. They ate through my stash of yarn in no time, and they were always looking for more needles. One of the girls came up with a great idea. After a month of advertising the swap for them, I took them to the farmers' market with whatever knitting they had finished and we set up a needle exchange. We put a bucket out and people would put a pair of needles in the bucket for a raffle ticket. Dozens of yarn companies and knitters donated yarn and the kids put together baskets of yarn with needles and notions to raffle off. You should have seen them...so proud of their accomplishments when they handed over their prized knitting."

I look at the clock and the shop is closing. I have to stop at the store on the way home. "Did you stay in touch with any of them?"

"For years I would get phone calls whenever one of them would get a 'legit' job, or had a baby. As far as I know, everyone kept up the knitting. I would get calls for patterns or to help with a new project. It was the most rewarding thing I ever did."

I finish tucking the last end in on my hat, snip the tail, and toss it in my bag. "We should get going, it's after six. Thanks for sharing your story with us, Nance. I had no idea. That was awesome."

"It really was the best time of my life."

Knitting group is out of my neighborhood and I need to get something at the store, so instead of driving to the one I know, I stop at the first one I see. When I pull out of the parking lot, I drive past a twenty-something-year-old sitting cross-legged on the sidewalk leaning against the stop sign. His cardboard sign reads: "Hungry, homeless. Will work for money." I hit the brakes, pull a U-turn, and drive back into the lot.

He doesn't see me because his forehead is resting in his hands, but he looks up when I slam my car door and I see gentleness in his eyes when I hand him a five-dollar bill.

"Can I ask you a question?" I sit down on the sidewalk cross-legged in front of him. "First of all, if you want to make more money, you should take off your hat. People want to see who you are. Most people will drive right on by if they can't see your face."

He removes his tattered hat and reveals a head full of curly black hair. "See? Now you look approachable." A van stops and he gets up to accept the bills thrust out the passenger window. It's getting to be dinnertime and it's cooling off...probably why he has his hat on. He sits back down in his spot at the signpost and through his open jacket, I notice that his clothes are faded and worn, but clean.

"How much money do you make in a day?" This is not what I came here to find out, but manners aside, I'm curious.

"It depends." I should have known that he wasn't going to give me an income report.

"I really want to know how come you're homeless. Why are so many of you guys living on the streets? Are you a foster kid? Do you mind telling me?"

He says he doesn't mind. There are a lot of kids who want to be on the street because it's better than living at home. He's not a foster kid. He's homeless because his girlfriend left and he couldn't afford the rent by himself.

"I got messed up over it and lost my job."

"Why don't you just look for another job?" Oh, that sounds harsh. I wish I'd thought of a nicer way to ask.

"It's not that easy. Besides, I make enough money to eat. I plan on getting a job, but right now, there isn't much out there." I wonder how he gets his clothes cleaned.

"Where do you sleep at night?" I feel like I'm interviewing, but for five dollars, he doesn't seem to mind. A car stops and he gets up for another handout, and when he sits again, he puts his hat back on.

"My head is cold," he says. "Hey, you're good luck. I don't usually get two in a row. Where do I sleep? Sometimes I sleep at friends', but after a while, you wear out your welcome. Most of the time, I find places down under the bridge with the winos. It's not so bad when the weather is good, especially if you have a box. When it's cold though, it sucks."

I stand up and dust the sidewalk off my jeans. I have to get home. "Well, thanks for talking to me. Take care of yourself, and good luck finding a job."

Another car stops and he launches himself off the cement. As I drive away, I think about him sleeping under the bridge, and then I wonder what I should make for dinner.

During my knitting time at home and the next three knitting groups, I work on the beanie hats, and today, as time runs out, I finish tucking in the ends on the last one.

"Pretty good, huh? Seven hats in four weeks," I brag to the girls. "I can't wait for my daughter to bring them to the guys. Can you imagine rowing on the bay every night without a hat? They must be freezing." I wrap my sweater a little tighter at the thought.

"I bet they'll really appreciate them," Nancy says. "See you girls next week?"

We all agree that knitting group is a much-needed activity. Maybe some of the others that we haven't seen in a while will show up now that the weather's cooler. It's hard to imagine that a few don't knit when the weather is warm. I need to knit every day. I toss the hat into my knitting bag and remember that I have to stop at the store on the way home. Shoot, I almost forgot. I'll walk down to the market at the end of the sidewalk instead. I hate stopping on the way home.

It's almost dark, but I recognize him as soon as I see the jacket, dark curly hair, and crossed legs. It looks like his sign is crumpled a bit and, as I get closer it appears that his clothes could use a wash. Shoppers walk around him as if he wasn't there, and I feel bad because there was a time when I would have done the same. I reach for my wallet and remember that I don't have a single dollar, and no change rattles in the bottom of my purse. Walking toward him, I make eye contact and he stands up.

"Dude...you moved."

He looks at me expectantly.

"What happened to your hat?"

"I took it off last week and forgot it. By the time I came back, it was gone."

"Bummer...Sorry, I don't have any cash."

"Oh." He blows a few hot breaths into his clasped hands, and then rubs his left hand across the top of his head.

"Here." I reach into my knitting bag. "Take this."

I can always knit another hat.

part five
Giving

chapter fourteen

Keep On Casting On

GALE AND I HAVE the kind of friendship where we're both busy at opposite ends of the day and if we don't call each other for a while, it's perfectly okay because we still care about each other. She called me one winter Saturday and told me that her sister just had an operation.

"Is she okay?"

"She's fine now, but she's sleeping and I don't want to leave her. You're going to laugh, but the reason I'm calling is that I ran out of yarn. I've been here for a few days and I finished my socks. I don't have anything to knit with and I don't know where any yarn stores are."

"Where are you? I'll bring you something from my hoard upstairs."

"I'm at San Francisco General. Dress warm, it's freezing outside."

"Can you believe it? I know how to get there. I'll put something together and see you in an hour then. Do you need a pattern, too? What do you want to knit?"

"Just a ball of sock yarn will do, if you have one."

"Ha ha, very funny. So your sister's going to be okay then?"

"Yeah, she's okay for now, but we'll be here for a while. I'll tell you about it when you get here."

I get a bag for a few different colorways of sock yarn, a couple extra pairs of circular needles, a bag of pretzels, and a thermos of hot coffee. I can't imagine being somewhere without something to knit, especially waiting in a hospital. I grab my knitting bag on the way out the door...I might stay long enough to work on my shawl.

"Hey, Gale," I whisper. The door is open. Her sister is sleeping with monitors beeping and although the medicinal hospital smell reminds me of painful times, somehow I like it. The patient on the other side of the room has her curtain open, but she's asleep as well. Gale ushers me into the hallway and after a giant hug, fills me in on her sister's condition. She opens the bag of sock yarn and yelps a whoo-hoo, which wakes both her sister and the other patient.

"Oops. Come in and meet my sister. The other girl's name is Lorraine."

We tiptoe in and I introduce myself. Gale's sister, Toni, mumbles a drugged hello and drifts back to sleep. Lorraine, probably in her early fifties, is all the way awake and when she sees yarn in Gale's hands, she sits up in her bed.

"I've been watching your friend knit," she tells me.

Gale holds up her finished socks for me to see.

"I knit all the time. I would be knitting now if I could. Can somebody please get me a drink of water?"

I move the tray with the pitcher closer to Lorraine's bed and pour a cupful.

"Thank you so much."

"You're welcome." What a nice gal, she looks fine and I wonder what's wrong with her but I don't ask. Gale pulls a chair for me in between the two beds and casts on for a sock. Lorraine doesn't go back to sleep.

"My mother taught me how to knit," she says.

I decide not to knit. I should have known better than to bring a charted lace shawl to work on. Lorraine wants to talk.

"I just love to knit. I knit everywhere. I used to knit at christenings and birthday parties and family get-togethers. I knit baby jackets, wedding shawls, sweaters, and baby socks. I never went anywhere without a gift for someone on my needles. How would they know how much I care?" Lorraine's words drift away from us as she looks toward the window.

Gale pauses in mid-round on the cuff of her sock and leans over. "This is the most conversation I've heard in days."

Lorraine turns back and murmurs. "Even when things became too much and left me too tired, I still knit. I know my heart will just stop one day and that will be that. Knitting keeps me going, I don't want to leave a single piece unfinished...no single-sock syndrome here."

Gale and I grin at her and she coughs out a little laugh. I think Lorraine's drugs are working. Everyone we know has single-sock syndrome.

"All of the love that I put into knitting for other people keeps my heart beating with every stitch I make. And I love color, too. Nothing bland for me. I see no reason why baby things have to be pink and blue and yellow. I like oranges and purples and greens and gold. Color is everywhere. And socks. Socks should reflect the wearer's soul, not made to match their clothes."

Lorraine gets quiet for a second.

"So that's why I knit. I feel like I'm marking out my

life and my fight with every sock and sweater and mitten and hat. I'm always casting on something new."

"And you didn't bring your knitting?"

"I had to come here in a hurry, and I don't have anyone to call to bring me my bag. I thought I would be going home soon, but I guess not. Watching your friend knit has been a lifesaver." She looks at Gale's socks again and I have no problem knowing what to do.

"Just so happens I have an extra ball of silk and wool sock yarn and a pair of size two's." I fish them from Gale's bag. "I hope you know how to magic loop."

"Oh, yes. Yes I do," her voice cracks.

I hand her the yarn and needles.

"A little silk with the iridescence of a butterfly's wings is just the thing to bring alive a winter's afternoon."

The monitor taps out her heartbeat loud and steady as she casts on.

chapter fifteen

Diane's Story

I MET DIANE AT a knitting group that I started for the nurses in the cafeteria at a local hospital. Turned out that we had more than an old friend and knitting in common. She opened up to the group and revealed an amazing story of perseverance. I asked her if she would write it down and this is what she sent:

I began having panic attacks and was prescribed an antidepressant. I took a high dosage for years and I couldn't function without it.

When my mom was ten years old, her bipolar schizophrenic mother had surgery to remove a brain tumor, and after that, she was meaner than ever. My dad was terrified of his alcoholic father who beat him on a regular basis. Both my parents were the oldest of eight children, born during the depression and raised in poverty.

They moved away from home as soon as they were out of high school and barely knew each other before they married and had us kids. She drove him crazy and he drove her crazy. In many ways, they were so opposite.

I don't think they had any idea what to do with us, so they ignored us.

My father's depression was relentless. After a day of work, he would come home and just want to be left alone. He would retreat to his recliner and read the paper or a book, or if she nagged, he would argue with her. She wanted his attention, but as far as he was concerned, his wife's job was to cook dinner and keep us kids quiet and away from him. My mom was a quivering, unhappy sixties housewife who existed on cigarettes and Tab. She was bored and lonely. He knew about her affairs.

My mother wasn't able to hide her obsessive-compulsive behavior. I followed her around while she turned doorknobs, checking and rechecking things that I couldn't see. I followed her around like an invisible puppy, acting out for attention, telling lies, and making up stories so she would notice me.

Mom believed that if she kept the perfect house and cooked lovely meals, then my dad would pay attention to her and appreciate her efforts. He figured that she should be happy because he was working and she got to stay home. They just didn't like each other and rarely spoke but when they did, they bickered incessantly. It was like they needed a whipping post. At least they didn't hit us.

Mother busied herself around the house cooking and cleaning all day; our house was almost sterile. At night, if Mom was relaxed, she would sew on a dress or knit on a scarf or a hat. She taught me how to knit...I think it was before I went to kindergarten. I remember sitting by myself and making miles and miles of garter stitch. I made row after row on a green scarf. It kept me out of the way and out of trouble. When I got older I tried sewing, but the needles were sharp and I was always poking myself. I loved to draw with pencils and paint with brushes. I liked all the artsy stuff. When I made something, my mother would look at it and notice me, and she might say I did a good job...or she would look at me and not say anything. Nothing.

When I was ten, my parents divorced and my father left our home in California to start a new family, repeating history with an unhappy wife and more unwanted kids.

I was twelve when I got my first job. I babysat for Mom's best friend, Betsy. We were next-door neighbors, so she knew us kids well. To me, she was a super mom. She was outspoken about how talented she thought I was with my crafting. She said I was like Martha Stewart and could do anything. I liked it when she told me that, I liked it when she showed interest in what I was making. She told me that I was a very good cook. Her kids ate up everything I made. I was a real person when I was at Betsy's, not invisible, like at home.

I was a horrible student and failing in school...there were no expectations. At the beginning of high school, I simply stopped going. Nobody said a word. No concern, no push. The only thing that got me a grain of attention was my artsy stuff...drawing, painting, pottery, needlework, even cooking. If there was something to make with my hands, I wanted to do it and wouldn't give up until I figured it out.

Disconnected and depressed, Mom married again and again, but they ended badly because of her affairs. I hated watching her flail around with all those men.

There was always food in the refrigerator, but little interaction. No family dinners, no movies, no popcorn, no joy. My mother's romantic interests pushed us away even further and we were left to fend for ourselves. She was so weird in her own head; bummed out so much of the time that she never saw her teenage girls drinking, doing drugs, and having sex. She knew we were doing that stuff but she never said or did anything. She barely had a pulse. I was drawing, painting, sewing, smoking pot, acting out. I always had some sort of a craft to feel good about. Crafting was my only talent. It was the only thing that made me feel special.

As soon as my sister and I turned eighteen, we were totally on our own. My getting pregnant at nineteen barely got a nod.

I knit a teeny baby cardigan and a pair of booties. I went to Donna Dae's in Montgomery Village, got a pattern and some yarn, and figured it out on my own. It was my first real knitting after those miles of garter scarf and I was proud of myself.

When my baby was six months old, her father walked out. We fought over her for the next twelve years. I wish I still had that little outfit.

My medication ride was a nightmare. I was totally unaware of what I was really taking. I thought it was an antidepressant. The battle over custody of my daughter nearly killed me. Her father was filthy rich and I looked like shit in court compared to him (the drugs will do that). My daughter decided to live with her dad (he bought her) and I was devastated. I was crushed. I blamed my folks for everything. I wanted to kill myself. While hospitalized for severe depression, I met Gloria.

Her office was beautiful and comfy. I think she must have been in her late sixties or early seventies, from Chile. Kind and warm, she was the mother I wish I had. She looked like my grandmother and had eyes so brown they were almost black. She was four-foot-something, and about as big around as she was tall and gave the best hugs. She gave me great advice for how I could get through my addiction to pharmaceuticals, my custody situation, my job that I hated, my issues with my parents, my envy of my dear sister and how well she seemed to be doing compared to me, my abandonment issues, and she helped me get out of my toxic relationship.

My mom did do me one great service. She paid for me to see Gloria and for that I am grateful.

After therapy with Gloria and a good antidepressant, my life began to change. I stopped blaming, took responsibility, and finally grew up.

I started knitting again after I saw a woman knitting in the break room at work. I was married and isolated, living in the mountains an hour and a half from a yarn shop, but through books and the Internet and trial and error, I bought yarn and patterns and figured them out on my own. I was happy again.

I married a sober alcoholic, who stayed sober for only a year. I wish I knew what the trigger was, but he drank like he wanted to die. Not just a binge, not just to get drunk, but he drank to end the world. After arrests, jail, blackouts, and hit-and-run accidents, he would clean up, start the business over again, and dive back into the bottle. I filed for a divorce and then he went missing. For forty-five days. I was worried sick. Two young neighbor kids found him in the forest that backs up to our property. He was dead.

No one could tell me what happened, other than he'd been dead for probably a month...an alcohol-related heart attack, maybe, due to detox, or he drank himself to death. It was the saddest, scariest time of my life.

I had to sell his business, pack the entire house, get rid

of stuff and sell it. I had help, but I had to make decisions and organize on my own, all on the heels of losing him. My life was totally changed. I felt like I was vibrating. I was heartbroken, stressed out, and worried about money. I had two big dogs and worried about finding a home to rent that would allow me to keep them. I was in shock and mourning over my loss. The only thing that brought me joy and peace was knitting. It was the only thing that didn't make me sad or remind me of everything that I already lost or was about to lose. I was a manic knitter at that point and was knitting every second that I was not running around like a chicken with my head cut off trying to deal with my "new" life. I started meeting other knitters and a whole new world opened up. Sadly, I was unable to sell my home and had to give it back to the bank. I packed my entire world and put it in storage. My dear sister offered my dogs and my knitting stuff and me a place to stay, so I could just recover.

I couldn't focus to read or watch TV and was too devastated to socialize much. Knitting was meditative, and while at my most nervous, I could find calm and get a lot of knitting done. I relished and mastered the most complex patterns that I could find and making beautiful things helped me feel better.

I went to work, saved money, knit up a storm, and the healing began. The process of figuring out new patterns has helped me focus and really understand the craft. Knitting challenges me, and that makes my head explode with happiness. I'm able to create something that I thought I'd never be able to do. I surprise myself.

I am here. I am happy. I found love again and I'm knitting more than ever.

Totally dependent for many years, Dad was ill with Parkinson's disease and my sister and I cared for him right up until he passed away in 2011. I know he was proud of us and grateful for our care. He told us, and I am grateful that I could be there for him.

My mother is just beginning to decline. She is not quite at the point of needing our care and she is married again and I am not sure what the future holds. She is very secretive. We are close in some ways—knitting, cooking, and gardening—and when she is happy, she is delightful. When she's not, well...she's my mother.

chapter sixteen

Keep Fighting

DEBBY IS IN THE emergency room wanting out of her skin.

Monitors beep out her elevated heart rate, loud and steady. Metal rings scrape the curved rod surrounding her bed as blue curtains open to announce the arrival of the doctor. Debby is exhausted and barely able to speak. A nurse places a paper thermometer under her tongue.

The doctor asks if she's suicidal and she says no, but it's a lie.

Fifteen minutes after they got off the school bus, three of Debby's family members were tied, gagged, and stabbed to death in their home by a man who lived six houses down the street. Then he set their house on fire. Stabbed and tortured, their mother was found in the swimming pool with burns over eighty percent of her body. She was alive.

The doctor diagnoses Debby with post-traumatic stress disorder. He hands her a prescription and a list of therapists and sends her home, but there's nothing there.

I knew Debby all through high school. She was

shy and quiet...I was the troublemaker. We didn't have anything in common, or so I thought, until I read her letter:

I've never been in love, even though I was married for thirty-four years. Only two people loved me uncondi-tionally—Grammie, my father's mother, and Grampie Fonzi. Even though I lost them when I was in my twen-ties, my therapist says they're probably the only reason that I'm not full of hate, or a druggie, or an alcoholic. The rest of my family was not so lucky.

My mother taught me to knit when I was eight but I can't remember the event. I feel like I should remember such a sharing time, but I don't. Spending time with my grandmother is what I remember the most.

Grammie and I would sit in her living room together and she would let me untangle the balls of yarn from the basket at her feet. We would sit for hours and talk while she knitted clothes without patterns for old dolls that we found at a flea market. We scrubbed them and cut their hair sometimes, to make them pretty. We talked about God, and life on the farm, and my ancestors. Grammie knew about so many things.

We made rectangles that she stitched together for sweaters and she taught me how to sew a skirt that would twirl. Grammie knit dresses with ruffles and stripes and polka dots and she let me play with all the colors of the rainbow from the basket at our feet.

We placed the dolls in their knitted clothes like jewels in velvet boxes and wrapped them in shiny paper and then we sent them to poor children who lived on an Indian reservation in Oklahoma. Grammie said that the children there had no presents and they would be happy to get our dolls. It made me feel good to make something special for someone else. Even when I couldn't be with Grammie, I practiced my knitting so that someday, I could send dolls to poor children.

I got married too young, but that's what happened back in the seventies when you wanted to get away from home.

Walter was charming and witty and I fell head over heels, but as soon as we got married, things changed. Controlling and demanding, I became his property. I couldn't go anywhere or do anything without his permission, something he rarely gave. I felt like a prisoner and it was maddening because there wasn't a thing I could do about it. I had no support from my parents and no one to talk to.

He worked with his uncle as a mechanic and soon after we got married, he got laid off. I had to find some kind of work. The only thing I knew how to do was knit, so I took a job at a yarn store. My main job was to knit rag sweaters—raglan sweaters made from all of the left-over scraps. There were so many textures and colors and I loved knitting them. The owners of the store wanted me to learn to knit sweaters on a machine, nice office clothes, they said, but I wouldn't use the machine. I can't tell you how proud I was when they sold my first rag sweater at Bloomingdale's.

Walter joined the military. It was hard to leave the shop behind, but if Walter wanted to move, we moved. I packed up every bit of my yarn and needles and we moved overseas to Spain.

We lived on the eighth floor of a huge apartment building off base, with the luxury of a small propane oven, but no phone or television. I needed to find something to do so when the building security gave a thumbs-up, I would slip out of the apartment and walk quickly past the gate to the base. Uniformed guards patrolled all day and night and I hated the sight of the automatic machine guns hanging off of their shoulders. I was glad to be protected, even though I found out the only time we weren't safe was the two weeks in August when the Gypsies came to sell their horses.

On the way to the base, at the side of the road, an old woman motioned me over to buy her brightly colored hand-knit baby clothes, but I never stopped long enough to get a good look. She reminded me of Grammie.

After a few weeks, I brought some yarn and needles to the base to teach knitting to anyone who wanted to learn. Some of the men said they found it "manly." I think it was creative and relaxing for them, actually. Getting home wasn't relaxing, though. If the Spaniards were at the gate taking their flag down, I had to wait, which wouldn't have been so bad if I didn't have to go to the bathroom. We were expecting.

Walter had said it would be a wonderful idea to start a family, but as soon as I told him that I was pregnant, he blew up, said I betrayed him, the same way he asked for broccoli for dinner and when I served it to him, he said he hated broccoli, and he threw it across the table at me and wanted to know why would I be so stupid to buy it.

I didn't care if he thought I betrayed him, I was happy at the prospect of a new beginning, a family. I spent months pouring my love into every stitch of a snow white christening gown.

Once we were back in the states, our little girl was born and things got better for a while. A friend convinced me to enter the christening gown in the state fair. The best in show ribbon it received was not just pinned to the dress, it was pinned to my heart.

Walter took a job for a trucking company and left me home alone most of the time. I was almost grateful to be living most days as a single mom.

Money was tight, so I got a part-time job knitting sweaters, for a woman named Marta, who lived on a small farm. She owned two brown and white llamas, and when I would call to them, their long banana ears would flop when they ran to the fence. When I rubbed their noses, they hummed at me like a couple of purring cats.

The llamas' fur wasn't for spinning, though. Marta had a local sheepherder make her yarn. Her husband would take colored pencils and graph paper to the library and, after researching folklore patterns, he would chart them in color on the graph paper. My job was to knit a sweater from his charted designs, and if they liked the sweater, a photographer from New York would come down to take a picture. The pictures and pattern directions were either made into a kit, or sent to England and knit by women there. They put one of my sweaters on the cover of a book once, but my name never got published because they said it was a cottage industry. It's a happy and creative time for me, and I loved visiting Marta and the llamas on the farm.

Just when I thought things were almost perfect, Walter takes a new job for a different trucking company and, this time, we have to move all the way to Florida. He's still away during the week and home on the weekends, which makes me happy because it gives me a much-needed break from his tyranny. I knit, and I relax, and I read. I think about our daughter away at school, and I think about Grammie.

Florida has warm weather most of the year, but on this day it was especially perfect. It was six o'clock and I had a few new friends over and we were sitting on the front porch when a neighbor from two doors down walked up to my porch with a couple of bottles of beer in his hands and said hi. I didn't know him, but he'd been in my house once or twice when my husband was home. He just stood there.

"Looks like girl talk going on here," he says. I'm relieved when he walks away.

At eight o'clock I hear a knock at my front door. I'm too nice. I let him in.

He's drunk. He sits down and starts talking sex. I usher him outside as quick as I can and notice a wet spot on my lounge chair. How long has he been sitting out here?

I try to get him to leave the deck, but he knocks me to the ground and pins me down. I struggle against the weight of him and push him off of me, but when he stands up, he whips around and grabs my elbow. I thrash from side to side and shake his grip loose and I run. I don't run fast enough, though, because he catches me. He catches me over and over again for the next three hours and no one hears my screams.

When the police question him, he says it must have been a misunderstanding. He says it was my fault. I can't go outside, I can't think, I can't breathe. I hide in my room for days.

Walter was due home for a long weekend, and everyone would know soon, so I had to tell him. He said that it was my fault because I always go around hugging and kissing everyone. I never even shook this guy's hand. I tell Walter that I want to move...I really need to move, but Walter says it's too much trouble to change our address and I tell him I'm drowning in a fishbowl.

That's when I get the news about the murder of my relatives in Connecticut, and I can't take any more.

I pack my yarn and my life and my PTSD into a moving van and drive away.

I still have trouble concentrating, but I'm getting better. Last year, I knit ten different sweaters for my grandchildren—there isn't a knitting pattern that I can't figure out. I have a new grandbaby on the way and I found some pink and purple Debbie Bliss yarn in my stash. It'll be perfect for a little sweater with a matching cap and booties.

This year, my daughter wants to pass on our legacy and make things for those less fortunate. My granddaughters are asking about Grammie's dolls. They want to learn how to knit. I'm looking forward to seeing them and spending time with my family. And now I know where it is I need to go. I'm loading up everything I own for one last move. I'm going home.

part six
Discovering

chapter seventeen

The Suitcase

BILL AND LAURA WERE expecting for the fourth time. Losing their first three babies through miscarriage devastated them both. Each month of pregnancy felt like an excruciating eternity. Laura needed to keep her mind occupied as she prayed to have one baby to keep.

She knit bootie after bootie, each stitch matching the ticking of time until booties multiplied and tumbled out of their box, too many pairs for one baby to have. Always praying, she made layettes, blankets, hats, mittens, sweaters, more hats, and even more booties. Laura told me that she made them in lemon yellow, mint green, pale pink, baby blue, and white; some had hearts, others had ribbons and bows.

"This baby would know how much love I put into every precious piece," she said.

It was Easter when Matthew was stillborn four months early. Bill closed Laura's hospital suitcase and wheeled his crying wife to the car. The drive home was silent, except for the wrenching sobs from the passenger seat.

A few months later, Laura, although still grief-stricken

and depressed, knew she needed to move on. "It was a warm, summery day when I packed up the baby clothes and blankets. It was so hard to let go, but I wanted them out of the house. I just couldn't face having them as a constant reminder of our baby who would never get to wear them.

"I took them to the hospital where Matthew was born, to the maternity ward and asked the first person I saw if they knew any new mothers who might need clothing for their baby."

The nurse directed Laura to a single room occupied by a young teen mother. Laura knocked lightly then peeked around the open door.

"Hello?" The occupant didn't answer, but Laura tiptoed into the room with her cache of baby clothes. A young girl sat in bed in tears. Even before she introduced herself, Laura asked what was wrong.

"I think I'm gonna have to give my baby up for adoption, and I don't know if it's the right thing to do," she wails, and buries her face in both hands. At a loss for words, Laura stands by the side of the bed and gently strokes the girl's hair.

"Let me share a story with you," Laura says, pulling her suitcase and a chair next to the bed. As Laura speaks, she opens the case and places each baby item, one at a time on the bed, smoothing and caressing each one. The young mother sits up a little straighter to see, her tears continuing to fall unchecked. While Laura tells her story, they both fixate on the beautiful knitted clothing that soon covers the entire bed.

Laura, now in tears herself, tells the young mother how it felt to lose all of her babies, and how badly she wanted the last one to make it.

"What was your baby's name?" the girl asks Laura.

"Matthew. His name was Matthew."

It's a blustery winter day thirty years later, and Laura is shopping at her local grocery store. She's waiting in the checkout line when a young man, cradling a baby in one arm and pushing a cart with a toddler strapped into the seat, gets in line behind her.

She catches a glimpse of them and the pain of loss she thought long gone now wells in the back of her throat. Laura grabs a magazine from the rack to divert her attention but the baby gurgles and she can't help but turn her head. Something about the baby and the little boy catches her off guard. She stares at them in wonder, and then it hits her. They're both dressed in clothes that look identical to the ones she knitted for her baby so many years ago.

"Excuse me, sir, your children are adorable. Can I ask about their cute clothing?"

The man smiles. "My mother had a huge collection of knitted baby clothes given to her a long time ago and she passed them on to me for my children. In fact, I wore them when I was a baby."

He shifts the gurgling baby to his other hip and pats the toddler on the head. "I have a whole suitcase full." Laura's face turns pale and her eyes start to water. The man asks her if she's okay and she nods silently.

"I haven't introduced us," he says. "These are my boys, Trent and Simon." He looks at them lovingly. "And my name is Matthew."

chapter eighteen

Vision of Change

MAJESTIC HERITAGE OAKS SCATTER throughout the campus. Due to the parking dilemma, I'm hours early for my photography class, but I don't mind because two hours gives me plenty of time to do my favorite thing under my favorite tree.

It's a little chilly for spring, but the sun moves through the mossy branches, casting its warmth on the wooden bench. Rats, there's already somebody there, but I can see that she's knitting. Perfect!

"What are you making?" I ask, as I walk toward her. It's a common question among knitters.

"Hi." She smiles but doesn't look up. "I'm working on a sweater for my mom."

I sit in the sun at the other end of the bench and pull out my project. "These socks are for me. I'm finally making something for myself. I love your colors."

"Thanks. I'm Lydia." She extends a hand in my direction, but it doesn't quite reach me. Odd, I think, until I see a white cane leaning on the bench to her right.

"I'm Lee. It's nice to meet you." The words hesitate to form properly. Is she blind for real? I reach for her hand and give it a gentle shake.

An awkward silence follows. I close my eyes and force my hands to make a stitch in the darkness. The needle misses the entrance and the yarn wraps around the wrong point. Then I have to know, so I ask.

"I learned to knit when I was young," she answers. "I taught myself from books and after I got a little older, I'd go to the knit shop in my neighborhood where the owners would help me. No one in my family ever knit, so I have no idea how I got so absorbed in it all, but I've knitted for years. I knit things for my family and friends then I knit for my friend's friends. I knit for my neighbors and their kids, and then I knit for the neighborhood dogs."

We both laugh. I know about the plight of the knitter who has too many knitted things and not enough people who want them.

"When there was no one else to bestow my gifts upon, charity knitting seemed the logical solution because I was never going to stop knitting. Are you taking a class?"

"I'm taking a photography class, just for fun, although if I'd remembered that school means tests and homework, I might have thought twice."

She laughs again, and then a quiet stillness saturates the air. Lydia places her knitting in her lap and lifts her head in contemplation.

"I was into photography and visual arts...and then this." Her left hand flutters in front of her eyes, as if she's waving to herself.

I think maybe I should be minding my own business, but that never happens, so I probe for more. "What happened?" My curiosity has no mercy.

"Well," she says, as she picks up her knitting. "In my

early thirties, I was living my dream come true—I had finally earned a degree as a professor of fine arts and humanities. I took a sabbatical from teaching to do some research on medieval art and one night, I went to bed... I went to bed fine...and when I woke up, I was totally blind."

"Just like that?" Leaning closer, I squint into her blue eyes and try to see how they're broken.

"They said I had a mini-stroke that killed my optic nerves. When I heard that there was no treatment or cure, I was devastated, to say the least." I watch her knit perfect little stitches.

"No one knew what to do with me. Blindness rehabilitation is something that doctors don't know anything about. They diagnose you then send you home to figure out how to live without your eyes. My whole world changed in an instant. I thought it was pretty much over. I couldn't tell if it was night or day and the simplest tasks were impossible. How would I cut my nails? How do you get toothpaste on a brush? How do you put makeup on? I didn't know if I'd be able to make a cup of tea or dial the phone. I didn't know if I would ever use a computer again and it totally freaked me out. For five months, all I did was lie in my bed and listen to books on tape. I never wanted to get up again."

I don't want to be late for class, but I can't leave now. "How did you get to be such a good knitter?"

"Well, it took a long time for me to even try." She doesn't miss a stitch.

"I still remember the day. It was dismal and winter. I know because I could smell the dampness and the snow. I sat in my soft, velvety recliner with my feet extended on the footrest and, as usual, my eyes were closed. Keeping them closed helped me center myself and relax as best I could. The strain of trying to see was so overwhelming that I would suffer from excruciating headaches. I was so aware of the connection. My brain would try so hard to see things, but my body just wouldn't do it. I spent most days in bed trying to cope with it all, the pain, the loss, the anger, and frustration. Then one day, something just snapped." Lydia puts her perfect knitting in her lap and turns her head in my direction.

"I thought about the sweaters I'd been knitting for needy kids. I was thinking about them, and how I longed to be able to finish the pink one that I started. Maybe, just maybe, I might be able to knit again. A huge desire to finish just that one consumed me. It was the first time in what seemed like forever that I felt anything remotely resembling excitement."

My pulse races with anticipation.

"I found the bag with the half-finished sweater and the yarn. The yarn felt so incredibly soft, probably worsted weight. I sat there with the fiber in my hands, so determined, holding my needles like this." She picks up the knitting from her lap and demonstrates.

"I couldn't remember the color of the yarn or the stitches I was supposed to be making, but I could feel it, and all of a sudden, I remembered the joy that if nothing else in my life was going right, I always had my knitting. I remembered being one with the yarn and the motion, and I would knit the hours away. It was a place I went, a place outside of myself." I know what she means. I know the joy place.

"I struggled so hard. I tried and tried, but I just couldn't do it. In the pitch black, it was always the sting of failure. I really wanted to find that place again. And then, after a ton of tears and meltdowns, I realized I couldn't do it because I was trying to see it. Well, since I couldn't see it, I closed my eyes and tried to feel it. My fingers would be my eyes. I hadn't thought of it that way. I started feeling my way through, and even though it was incredibly hard, it was heaven!

"I knitted my way through rehab and the hard days, through the struggles and the depression. I learned how to put my patterns on a sound device so I could carry them with me and I knit everywhere. I got my confidence back, I got my pride back, and I was able to let go of all that self-doubt and fear. Things got better, and I finished that pink sweater...and then I donated it."

I wish she could see the smile on my face. It's time to go so I toss my untouched sock into its bag and get up from the warm bench.

"It was so nice to meet you, Lydia." I rest my hand lightly on her shoulder. "Do you live around here?" I hope to knit with her again.

"I live close enough to walk. I come here pretty much every day to knit and take pictures."

"Wha...?" Before I can ask, she tells me how she finds a tree, feels around the trunk, and points her camera up through the canopy.

"I'm still a pretty darn good photographer, too."

chapter nineteen

Shed Full of Treasure

STANDING ON THE BRIDGE, I see a yellow dog bouncing through the water, crazy, like he's chasing a rabbit. It's Jeanette's dog, Shoji. I always meet the neatest people while walking my dog. How lucky Shoji is to run free, I think, as I have to keep my Zena leashed. Her "labitude" and selective hearing keeps her tethered to a sixteen-foot retractable leash. I would love to let her run with Shoji, but if I asked her to come, she would tip her head and wag her tail and laugh at me and not listen. This, I know from experience. Shoji bounds up the steep bank through the blackberries and onto the bridge. He gives Zena a kiss.

"Weird weather, huh?" Jeanette asks as we walk across the bridge. The clouds are dark and heavy with rain and when the sun pokes through them, spindles of gold fall onto the ridges behind the hills. I can feel the change, something different on the inside, like wind and storm and excitement, like I felt when I was little. In the distance, I think I see a flash of lightning.

I remember the day perfectly. I sat on my rock and picked mossy pieces of pale green lichen, rolled them up, and tossed them into the wind. Giant puffs of gray clouds hung across the darkening sky.

With two clothespins poking from her mouth, Mother bent over and pulled a wet sheet from the wicker basket and snapped it on the breeze before attaching it to the line. "These should be dry in no time," she said. She noticed me watching her and then she looked up at the sky.

The clothesline was down the hill and off to the side at the lower edge of the backyard. It was my favorite place to play. Long stretches of white rope hung between telephone-pole trees waiting for clothespins, like little wooden dolls, to pinch and hang our wet clothes and hand-knit sweaters.

"Yes, the wind is picking up." She looked off through the woods over the tops of the trees toward the ocean. When the basket was empty and Mother was gone, I flew between the rows of fresh-smelling towels and bleached sheets, slapping every wet piece with the palms of my hands.

In the morning, I had to go to school. A big yellow bus picked us up down the hill at the stand of mailboxes next to the beach. I would search for colored sea glass while the other kids waited where they were supposed to, at the mailboxes, and most days I went to school with sand in my shoes.

The wind rattled an open classroom window and the tops of the trees twisted and bent. The principal, Mr. Thomas, made an announcement but I didn't listen, and the teacher said we can all go home now, but it was still morning and I didn't get to read. I practiced reading and I was good at reading so I wanted to read. See Spot run.

We bounced around and hollered like we always did, but the bus driver kept his eyes in the mirror instead of turning his head around. He almost always turned his head around and yelled at us. When the bus rounded the corner to the causeway, where cattails explode and rubies grow in the rocks, there was nothing but water. The bus stopped very fast with a squeal and a hiss and my papers fell off my lap and I had to squeeze under the seat in front of me. As soon as I picked them up, I looked out the window and my mother was waiting at the bus stop. I must be in trouble. I didn't know why she was there, because my sister and brother and I always walked home alone. The yellow accordion doors opened and she scooped us into a huddle against the wind. Her clothes were wet. Wind whipped my ponytail into my eyes and I could hardly stand up straight. Mother looked from the bus to the road, the road that used to be there, and I didn't know how we're going to get home. The ocean had come and swallowed the road.

"It's a hurricane." Her face was pale. "We have to get home. You kids remember when I taught you how to swim, right?" She held us around our waists while I tried to keep my lunch box over my head. We waded into the causeway.

Later that night, windows rattled with thunder, and rain smashed into the house. Mom let me sit very close to her while she knit on a sweater by candlelight and then a crack of lightning split the sky and sent me crawling into the darkness under my bed.

Back on our walk a rumble of thunder follows the flash and Jeanette and I decide to leave the bridge and continue on. A neighbor jogs by with a stroller and Zena pulls on her leash.

"Do you still want to teach me to knit?" Jeanette asks. We talked about knitting the last time we met.

"Of course, I'd love to. How about we meet at my house? Shoji and Zena can play in the backyard and we can hang out on the deck. I have a ton of yarn and needles. Didn't you say you already know how to crochet?"

"I learned when I was young, but never made much of anything with it. The only other person in my family who crocheted was my mother-in-law, but she died soon after I met my husband. When she passed away, I helped to clean out their shed and found a whole bunch of her knitting and stuff. There were bags of unfinished crocheted blankets and a huge stash of yarn. With all of my excitement over the find, my father-in-law said I could have it all, and I knew right then and there that I would try to finish those afghans for the kids. He told me she would have loved for them to be finished.

"I worked on them like crazy, it took more than a year, but I finished four of them and sent them to my nieces. It's been a long time. It seems like forever ago, before we moved here after Katrina."

"You were in Hurricane Katrina?" There's always a connection, every time I meet someone. How bizarre that she would mention a hurricane.

"I was visiting my husband's sister in Alabama when it hit. Nobody thought it would be as bad as it was. Neighbors were stuck on the roof of their store; they had a gas station on that side of the river and the water rose so high that it covered everything. My sister-in-law's house was further up the hill, above the surge. Our whole family stayed upstairs, crowding together while windows shook and water raged everywhere. I was scared to death. We lit candles and waited it out. The girls brought their blankets and we all cuddled together in the bathroom. I had all of my crochet stuff with me, so I taught my nieces how to crochet while we sat in the candlelight. It made things less scary for them, concentrating on making chains.

"When I got home, I found out that my husband was being transferred out here to California. I miss the girls, but I hear that they're still crocheting, and they still have their Grammy's blankets that I finished. They're actually coming for a visit next month. The oldest says she wants to learn how to knit, so I was hoping you would teach me so I could teach her."

The rain comes and Zena is lagging behind. We finish our trek around the creek and say goodbye at the bridge where we started. Shoji looks like he could go another two miles.

"If you meet me here next week, we can take a walk first and then knit." Shoji licks my hand while I inhale the scent of fresh rain on the pavement and think about having a new friend at my house.

It's a beautiful sunny day and we have a good time in the backyard. Jeanette is a natural; the transition from crocheting to knitting is easy for her. The dogs run crazy goofy in the yard around the deck and, after slurping a gallon of water, plop themselves in the shade. Jeanette tells me that she got a call from her niece.

"Aren't they coming for a visit soon?" I ask. "Is everything okay?"

"Oh, everything is fine. She told me that she went to a crafty thrift store place and found something totally cool. She was all excited on the phone. She found a knitted blanket that someone else had started but didn't finish, and it had all of the yarn and directions with it.

She bought it, because I said I would teach her to knit, but mostly, she said, 'because it was someone's treasure and I want to finish it so I can find it a home and pass on the love.'"

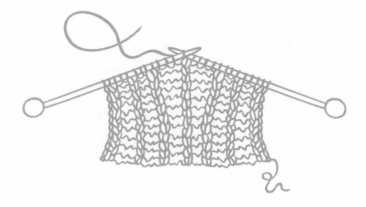

part seven
Living

chapter twenty

Wicker and Lace

ROBERT AND I MET several times while knitting together at a bookstore in town and he talked at great lengths about his dream of opening a yarn store. He was mild-mannered and kind, and I enjoyed our discussions on what might be the pros and cons of owning your own shop. (I think it's every knitter's dream.) I didn't see him for a few weeks and was sad to learn that he moved suddenly to care for a sick friend. We lost touch over the years but when Robert messaged me that he was back in town, he asked if the group was still knitting.

I told him that I would love to have coffee, and no, the bookstore closed.

While I ordered our mochas he secured a comfortable corner table and when I sat down, I asked him how he'd been, what he'd been doing.

"I finally opened my own shop," he said.

"Oh, do tell me everything! Tell me the whole story." He was charming as ever as he told me how he found the shop.

"It all started when I saw a crooked 'For Sale' sign

on the front lawn of an old Victorian, just a few blocks from downtown on a large corner lot. It was in desperate need of a few coats of paint and the removal of a weedy, woebegone garden, but I fell in love the minute I passed the property and wondered why anyone would want to sell such a beautiful place.

"An old Victorian would be perfect for a yarn store, I thought, a charming and natural fit for the neighborhood. The large bay windows in the front sealed the deal. A yarn store needs big windows."

"Oh, yes, I agree."

"The house was in need of some serious TLC, so I painted the old clapboards a cream color with mauve trim and a welcoming red for the front door. My dear friend, David, gifted us a weeping cherry tree that we planted to the left of the path leading to the front steps where visitors could sit and look over the curves of the canopy and watch people stroll on the sidewalk. He gave us a trio of young river birches that we planted in a kidney shape to the right of the entry path, near a dense row of burning bushes that ran along the property line on the north side. Sadly, after a long battle, David passed away a few weeks later. The trees became a memorial planting...a gift that would live on, he said."

Robert sets his coffee down and stares at the trees across the parking lot before continuing.

"Under the shadows of those ancient oaks, we had a lush and lovely garden of bleeding hearts, lilies of the valley, coral bells, and ferns. Customers would gather on the porch to drink sweet tea or an occasional glass of wine and we knit for hours, sometimes late into the evening. It was a glorious place."

"It sounds wonderful." Robert brings a sock out of his

bag, so I pull out my shawl. We both agree that our knitting is fabulous. "Tell me more."

"Well, one sunny afternoon, while I was watering the garden, an elderly couple greeted me from the sidewalk. I invited them to the front porch for an iced tea and learned that they were the original owners of the house, retired, looking for a small rental, and had been married forty-five years.

"It just so happened that the whole upstairs was set up for renting, I think they knew that. I had the master room off the back of the downstairs. They were moved in by the next week.

"Max and Dottie were the perfect tenants. I never heard a peep from upstairs. Occasionally, I would see them under the cherry tree or in the garden holding hands. Dottie was a lovely lady with brown shoulder-length hair and a rather thin, small frame. She had a rare, warm, and disarming smile, which was naturally contagious, and Max wore the same smile when they were together. They were the sweetest couple.

"Dottie told me how happy she was to be back in her old Victorian. She loved the new red door, turquoise hallway, bulletin boards, yarn, colors, and textures. The antique built-in china hutch housed specialty yarns, and sample sweaters hung on the open wood and glass doors. Books signed by their designers stacked on top of the hutch for customers to enjoy. I would let them look, but I wouldn't sell them.

"Thursdays were Knit Nights. Every week, music and laughter poured out of the open plantation windows. Alice, our local hairdresser, was always the first to arrive. She brought her saggy basset hound George, who kept a sleepy vigil on the front porch. Some nights, he would lift his head to announce the arrival of a guest, especially Marsha, who usually brought a platter of the most decadent chocolate chip cookies. Other times, the thump of his tail on the wool-braided rug was all that he could muster. He always got a pat on the head, though, and I was very sure that he ate more than his share of cookies, judging by the looks of him. Alice was in the process of knitting him a sweater and although we told her that it probably wouldn't fit, she plodded on, assuring us that he would lose weight if we all stopped giving him treats!"

Robert tells me that there was never a Thursday night without a delightful gathering at the table in the middle room with the key lime walls, the white trim, and cherry wood shelving.

"The welcome mat was always out," he says after a sip of cold coffee.

"Sounds delicious."

"One morning, I was watering the hanging baskets and plants on the front porch, and Dottie appeared with a serious look on her normally gentle face. I knew that she was having some back issues but she looked especially bothered. Initially, I suspected Knit Night was too loud as it ran well past ten o'clock with a great deal of music and laughter. I was ready for some words of displeasure when she smiled and asked me if I would mind teaching her to knit. Whew, I thought. Certainly, I could do that.

"She said she'd like to make a scarf for herself and then she said she'd like it to be red because 'red complements my skin tone and hair color.'"

Robert laughs and knits a few stitches on his sock. I haven't knitted much, as his story has me captivated.

"I agreed to teach Dottie to knit and we selected the

perfect chunky red yarn and bamboo needles. Dottie said that she likes the 'green' aspects of the bamboo. She would sit in front of one of the large bay windows, flanked by lace curtains in a white wicker chair with the light streaming over her shoulder onto her knitting as she worked along, doing what most new knitters do; making every stitch just so, just perfect, listening to music of the hour...nothing too sleepy...nothing too radical...sometimes as wild as Elvis or the Beatles."

"You're dating yourself," I say.

He raises an eyebrow and continues.

"When I asked Dottie why she wanted to learn how to knit, she told me, 'For the relaxation and fun...and it's so popular with so many celebrities like Julia Roberts.' I tried not to laugh out loud.

"Over the next few weeks I watched Dottie's red scarf grow. I remember leaning on the back of her chair and asking her what she liked most about knitting. I was surprised when she took only a second to answer, as if she'd already thought about it. She told me that knitting gives her focus and something to concentrate on. 'It's centering, like yoga,' she said, and it gives her something to take on appointments. Plus, she said, 'I get such a great sense of accomplishment and achievement from making something with my own two hands...not to mention the great people you meet. Knitting is such an icebreaker when you knit in public.'

"Everyone stayed to visit and knit with Dottie while her scarf grew. She was the light in the window, welcoming everybody as they came in the door. It wasn't unusual for Dottie to begin a conversation with everyone.

"In time, Dottie confided in me that she had an inoperable spinal tumor, and that learning to knit and visiting with folks kept her in the moment of joy and, most of all, kept her mind distracted from the pain. She told me how grateful she was for the gift I had given her. But I told her it was I who received her gift.

"Four, perhaps five, weeks passed. Dottie was thrilled that she had completed her scarf—a fine piece of knitting it was, a red scarf 'the color of the heart and love,' she said. The next day, I saw her teaching a new customer how to cast off. She was so proud."

Robert stretches and says that he should be getting back to his hotel.

"Wow, what a great story. Is Dottie watching the store for you while you're here, then?"

"We lost Dottie that week. At the next Knit Night, we all cried and then we laughed and then the summer night air blew through the bay windows and billowed the white lace curtains over the back of Dottie's wicker chair. Max was pleased when we hung her long red scarf there, a tribute to her and the gift that she left us all."

chapter twenty-one

Community

ONE OF MY FAVORITE flights to the east coast involves a layover in Charlotte, North Carolina, because they have plantation rocking chairs in front of gigantic plate glass windows. After a washup, a piece of the finest cheese pizza, and a Diet Coke, I settle in to a few hours of splendid, peaceful, uninterrupted, meditative lace knitting.

It never fails. Someone sits down next to me and wants to talk.

"What are you making?" The chart slips off of my lap and the note keeping my place floats to the floor beyond my reach.

"Oh, it's a lace shawl." I try to keep my annoyance at bay because I would do the same thing if I saw someone knitting at an airport. I know that knitters are drawn to each other—we are a community after all. With thirty-eight million of us, I'm bound to run into a knitter in the Charlotte airport.

"Do you knit?" I ask, while sliding my sticky note back to my chair with my foot.

"I do. I design and I knit to keep my hands moving.

I have thoracic outlet syndrome, which interferes with feeling and fine motor control. If I didn't knit, I'd break all the dishes."

I don't know what her disease is, but we both laugh. She introduces herself as Maryanne and I tell her my name.

"Don't you write patterns? I know your name. I've seen your patterns at Knit Picks and Patternfish and I saw your post about designing for Strings and Things in Hawaii. I love that Makena Sunset Shawlette you did with the owner's hand-dyed yarn. You're very talented!"

I think I'm blushing. Who knew? This is very cool. Wow, someone knows me for my knitting. I'm shocked.

"Nice to meet you, Maryanne."

We chitchat a little about where we're going and who we're seeing and how long we get to stay and knit. Looks like we're on the same flight out and we have two hours and fifty minutes. I change out my lace shawl for a sock so we can chat. She brings out a pink and brown striped hat on a circular needle.

"Mindless knitting for planes and airports."

"Very nice, always a good idea."

"So, when did you learn to knit?" I decide to ask her before she asks me. I'm tired and I would rather listen than talk.

"I learned from my mom, I must have been seven or eight, with white yarn, and big, straight needles. She taught me both knits and purls, and set me to work knitting stockinette stitch right away. I distinctly recall working about ten rows and then thinking there must be a better way, so I figured out how to knit backwards."

That's weird.

"Did you stay with it? I always wished I had through my childhood years."

"Knitting didn't really stick as a pastime, though I'd pick it up now and then and give it a go. I remember the beautiful sweaters and mittens my mom made. I can still see them in my mind's eye and I wish I had more of her work from that time. If I'd known then how important knitting would become to me, I'd have taken it a lot more seriously."

I notice that she knits a little awkwardly. Something seems a little different in the motion of her hands and she sees me watching.

"When I was fourteen, I took a header off my bike without a helmet. Broke my upper jaw and fractured my skull. I was out riding my new ten-speed bike that I'd babysat the entire summer to pay for. I'm not sure what happened but I remember going down a steep hill and I guess I went over the handlebars. I landed on my skull first, fractured it, then bounced up and came down a second time on my front teeth, smithering my upper jaw all the way to my nose. I have no bone in there at all, now. It's pretty amazing I look normal."

"I think you look great, I would have never known."

"Thanks."

I'm in a knitting and listening groove.

"It happened in front of a church. They called an ambulance and then everyone came out and circled around me, unconscious on the road. The priest started reading last rites over me and I woke up. I clearly remember that. I spent three weeks in the hospital, and the rest of the summer smearing antibiotic ointment on the skin I'd burned off. After that, I thought everything was fine except for the prosthetic teeth I have to wear.

Looks aside, I got married and had two fabulous kids, and that's when my knitting took off. You have kids?"

"Four, all grown."

"Then you probably know what I mean about knitting for kids; you must have had the best dressed kids if your patterns are any indication."

"Oh, I wasn't a designer back then, but I did make them a few things. Nothing like the stuff I design now, though." She's feeding my ego and I like it.

"I was big into mittens and hats. Then something really weird happened. One day, I couldn't maintain my tension while knitting on a pair of stranded mittens. This went on for a few weeks, my tension got worse and worse, even in garter stitch. Then I started cutting and burning my hands when I cooked. I just couldn't feel them. I went to the doctor and they told me I had a ton of scar tissue and nerve damage because of the accident. I was totally freaked out. I needed to knit."

"How did you get to where you are now? Your knitting looks perfect."

"Well, it took a while. I went through six months of bed rest and two years of physical therapy. I was dropping things all the time, but I was determined to knit. My tension was still terrible. I didn't try to make anything; I just knit. Every day. Miles and miles of yarn. It gave me peace, you know, that meditation so many of us find. And after a while my hands started to look more normal. You can't believe how my tension improved. I learned how to do things by muscle memory, and not on feeling. It was awesome. The more I knit, the more the feeling came back to my hands. I started to knit things again. Sweaters and mittens and hats. What a joy that was.

"Every day now," she says, "I swatch and write patterns and knit and design...because knitting is what gets me through."

I nod. We sit and rock and knit.

chapter twenty-two

Every Day

THROUGH A CONVERSATION ON the Internet, Peggy found out that I grew up on the east coast, designed and knitted children's clothing, and never rode a train. She wrote me to share this story about a special blanket:

Greg and I worked together at Mass Transit, Metro North. A big, easygoing, red-headed bear of a man with a ZZ Top beard and glasses, he would be the first one to tease you about something silly you said, or give you a helping hand if you needed one.

We ran the train yard—setting up trains for the morning rush hour, moving cars to the shop for repairs, and all of the other things yard duty workers do to keep the trains running. The conductor, engineer, and brakeman, our whole yard, in fact, clicked together. Like firefighters, we were a close-knit crew, often spending as many as twelve hours a day together. Greg was a good cook. But it can happen at any time, a change in job routes or home terminals or different hours can break up a crew and it might be years before you run into each other again.

Greg's wife had recently given birth to a baby boy, but something was wrong. Greg was pale with worry and visibly suffered while his wife and baby were in the hospital. The baby needed an operation, and the prognosis wasn't good.

I had planned to crochet a blanket for the baby. Years ago, I crocheted with cotton thread, attempting things like doilies and tea towel edgings, but never got very far. When a friend's wife gave me a box of mismatched yarn, I thought I'd use it for the blanket for Greg's new arrival. I didn't know much about yarn, but I liked the feeling of the colors and textures as they popped out of the box. I never progressed much past potholders, but I wanted to make this baby a blanket, to thank Greg for being such a special friend.

With the news that the baby might not make it, I had to hurry.

I gathered the yarn balls into a pile and began: greens for healing, yellows for warmth and sunshine, blues for serenity and peace, peaches and pinks for love, and red for energy. Those are the colors that wanted out. Each stitch that came off my hook said, "You will make it, little one...keep fighting. Everything will be fine." My heart ached as I crocheted long into the nights.

I didn't know about mixing yarns of different thicknesses and weights, so that might explain the lopsidedness, and although somewhat embarrassed, I was proud to have finished it. I wrapped it up with a note explaining what all of the colors meant and when I handed it to Greg, he hugged me tight and I knew from the bottom of my heart that the baby would pull through.

It was a rough couple of months. Nancy kept vigil over their baby, Tommy in the hospital while Greg returned to work. All of us in the yard looked for little ways to make him feel better. After talking to Nancy on the phone one day, he smacked his elbow on the doorjamb between the kitchen and dining room and it was more than just a tap. Seizing an opportunity, I took my double-jointed elbow and twisted it grotesquely, demonstrating how he might have been able to clear the side of the door and avoid the smack, if only he had the same ability to bend.

He cracked up. Greg laughed the kind of laugh that no one had heard in weeks.

He told me later that, had it not been for my silly antics, he might have broken down then. He told me that he was ready to fall apart.

The baby started showing signs of recovery, and Greg thanked us all with hugs and handshakes for helping him cope with it all. When little Tommy came home from the hospital, we got the best meal that "Dad" had ever cooked. Nancy sent me a beautiful thank-you note for the blanket, and another one for the crew, blessing us for keeping Greg together so she could keep her sanity.

Soon after, our crew broke up.

I saw Greg once in a while in passing and, after a hug, I would always ask him about his son.

"He loves his blanket," he would say, his huge beard grinning.

I was so proud of that blanket. It was my first big-yarn project and, even though it was a bit on the wonky side, I put all my love and prayers into it.

I kept crocheting and learned new things and my skills improved. For the last ten years, I've been a contract crocheter for different designers and a couple of yarn companies.

Then one day, I ran into Greg and Nancy.

"Peggy! How are you?" Greg's red hair was thinning and the beard was gone.

I ask about his son. I think about the blanket and cringe at the thought. It was awful, if only I knew then what I know now.

"He's quite the handsome young man, just like his dad." Greg's laughter echoes throughout the store.

Nancy steps closer to give me a hug. "He won't let me put it away," she says. "Tom still keeps that blanket folded at the bottom of his bed."

part eight
Sharing

chapter twenty-three

Crafty Ladies

IT'S TUESDAY AND I show up late for knitting group. Virginia looks like she's struggling to sew a bunch of knitted and crocheted squares together. Thirty-two of them in shades of blue cover the table in a checkerboard pattern. A few more knitters join us.

"What are you working on, Virginia?"

"Remember, I told you about the Crafty Ladies? We're putting together an afghan to raffle off at the crafts fair in November to raise money for more yarn. The ladies need more yarn so they can keep knitting for charity." I vaguely remember the mention, but as soon as I hear the words raffle and crafts fair I tune out. "Each one of the ladies made one of these squares. Some are new knitters and went way out of their comfort zone to do it, too."

Now this piques my interest. Making squares is not something I would volunteer to do, but out of your comfort zone is something I know about.

"Let me take a picture of the afghan. I'll try to write an article about you guys and to get you some publicity." The thought gets my adrenaline going and I stand on a chair to shoot a picture of the laid out squares. "I'll take a close-up of each square, too, so the ladies can have a record of which one they made."

"They'll be so excited to see this." Virginia walks around behind me, and watches while I shoot thirty-two pictures. Now I'm excited, too.

"You'll love the Crafty Ladies," she says. "I've told them all about you and how you have published patterns and teach knitting and they want to meet you. We meet on the third Wednesday of the month. Can you come next week?" She gathers up the squares in the proper order and sits at the other end of the table.

"I'll try, but it's hard to get away at that hour." If they want to meet me, I really want to go, but I'm afraid that I'll get lost, even with directions, because I always do. Just the thought causes my heart to race and I have to pat myself on the chest to calm myself down.

I think about the boxes of donated yarn filling my upstairs. I think about my offer to teach kids at a homeless shelter how to knit. The volunteer coordinator at the shelter told me last week that there might be as many as sixteen kids for the first group. I knew I didn't have enough smooth yarn in my stash, so I put out a call to my friends via the Internet for any leftovers or unwanted yarn. Seven hundred pairs of needles and twenty-two boxes of yarn showed up at my doorstep.

"Wait...I have yarn. I can bring yarn."

"That would be great, we sure can use it. We knit for eleven charities, and we can always use more yarn." Virginia probes her needle into a square and pulls a long blue piece of yarn through the edge. "That's why we're putting together this afghan, because we need more yarn." She grimaces with the next pull of the needle.

"Do you want me to sew it together for you? I love to

do the finishing work." With those words, all eyes from the group are on me. I always get that reaction when I say I love to sew things.

"Really? You want to do it?" Virginia is visibly relieved.

I alternate the light and dark blue squares and as I stitch them together, I wonder who made each one and why they would want to make something for somebody they don't know. Virginia sits opposite me and we both stitch the squares together.

Knitting club is over; it's time to go. Virginia safety-pins the squares in the proper order and I box them up to take them home.

"Thanks for doing this. You have plenty of time," she says. "The crafts fair isn't until November."

I hope the ladies don't mind a little dog hair.

I have two boxes of donated yarn in the front seat of my car, and even though I glance at the directions six times in twenty minutes, I overshoot the freeway exit and end up seven miles the wrong way. I'm sick with frustration, because this always happens, and now I'm late and I hate being late. They probably think I'm not coming. I eventually find my way back to the freeway and take the first exit but I'm all turned around. Wait, there it is. Somehow, I always end up where I'm supposed to be.

The auditorium off of the chapel is brightly lit and when I open the double doors, I'm hit with an explosion of color and textures. Rows upon rows of tables hold hundreds of knitted and crocheted blankets, hats, scarves, booties, quilts, and dolls. I am amazed. Other than the county fair, it's the most incredible gathering of knitting and crocheting that I've ever seen in one place.

The vision takes my breath away while the warmth of it pulls me into the room.

"We're having a showing for the congregation." Virginia greets me at the door and Carol, the head Crafty Lady, relieves me of the boxes of yarn that I forgot I had in my arms.

"Thank you, it's great that you could come," Carol says. "We've been looking forward to meeting you."

"This is the most incredible thing I've ever seen."

I still can't move. People mill about the tables admiring the handmade things. I smell coffee and Carol tells me to help myself to cookies and refreshments on the pass-through to the large kitchen. Her smile is as warm as the room.

"How many ladies made these? This is huge, there must be hundreds of things here."

"There's about twenty of us," Carol smiles. "We've made over five hundred blankets and lap throws, two hundred and thirty-seven hats, and a hundred and sixty-one scarves so far." She walks me over to a handmade poster with cutout photographs of the Crafty Ladies with a list of which items they've made for what charities. She picks up a see-through box filled to overflowing with neatly stacked baby hats in pastels of every shade with pom-poms the size of dimes.

"Wow, these hats are so tiny. They look like they would fit a doll. How cute are these?" I pick one out of the box to get a closer look; it's knit in the round with two-by-two rib. Yes, I could make these little preemie hats.

"We send them to Kaiser Hospital." Carol is glowing. "The parishioners want to see what we've made with the yarn they donate, so we're showing them today before we send the things out. As soon as we're through we'll pack everything up and deliver them to the charities." Holy mackerel, twenty ladies made all of these things and then they deliver them all over Sonoma County?

I attend the next get-together of the Crafty Ladies. I stand up and introduce myself and ask them if they would write on a piece of paper why they are here, and what knitting and crocheting for the community means to them. I want to write an article, I tell them.

"I was blown away when I walked in here and saw all of the beautiful things that you made. The community needs to know how special you ladies are, and how you give to others."

I tell them that I never thought about making things and just giving them away, giving a piece of myself to others. I tell them that I grew up thinking that the world owed me something, and that giving back wasn't something that I would ever do, and then I thank them for letting me be a part of something so special. I feel like they hugged my soul.

I don't have any knitting with me, but I want to make something while I'm here with the ladies. A look into the boxes of yarn spread out on the long table finds me a variegated bulky weight yarn in pastel colors and a size K crochet hook. I think I know how to crochet a hat from memory. I chain four, make a loop, and work eight single crochets into the loop and then I remember what I'm supposed to do next. When the circle gets to the right size, or what I think is the right size, I stop increasing, change to a solid color, and work the hat to the brim. The women are watching me like hawks, commenting on how fast I crochet, and wanting to know how I make a hat without a pattern. My head swells a little, and I'm a bit amused. I would think, with all the crochet that I've seen, that they would know how to make a hat. Come to think of it, most of the hats I saw were knit, so maybe they don't have a pattern in their heads.

"I'll be happy to write the pattern down for you." The words come automatically, because I want them to like me and I see lots of smiling faces, but I worry about writing a pattern that I made up the shaping for. I don't think I'll have time to work on it, but the next meeting is a month away so I should be able to give them something. Look at all they do for other people. I want to know what that feels like.

When I finish the hat, Carol brings me a Crafty Ladies tag and a pen.

"Sign it," she says, "and we'll add it to the bag of things going out."

My hand wobbles with excitement as I sign my name on the card. I feel something welling inside of me, something like I've never felt before.

At the next Crafty Ladies get-together, Carol hands me an envelope as soon as I set down a new box of yarn.

"I collected these for you." I forgot that I asked them to write something. "Thanks for getting the word out. We can use all the publicity we can get. We put out a small newsletter for the congregation, and an article would be great. I'll e-mail you some details about who we send things to, and how many we've sent."

At the next meeting, I crochet another hat and think about the child who might receive it and I feel good.

A week later I run into a friend of mine, Michelle, who used to knit with me at the yarn shop. We've always talked about getting a group together at the hospital where she works, and the timing is just right.

She makes a flyer to post on the hospital bulletin board to announce a once-a-week knitting group. The hospital cafeteria is brightly lit and the food is pretty good. We push a couple of tables together and our first Knit Night begins. I tell her about the Crafty Ladies and my upcoming group of kids that I'll be teaching at the homeless shelter.

No doctors show up, but we have a couple of nurses, including a guy (his knitting is the best out of the bunch), a mom and her daughter, an administrator, and myself.

I join the fun for only a few weeks. They don't need much knitting help, and it's time to start the kids' group at the homeless shelter. Three groups a week are more than I can handle, so I say good-bye to my friends at Kaiser, but not before I get to hand-deliver a bag of donated preemie hats from the last meeting of the Crafty Ladies. Just as I'm about to leave through the automatic doors, a new mom is being wheeled out past the front desk with a tiny newborn cradled in her arms.

"Wait, we have something for you." The lady at the desk places a basketful of baby hats on the counter and the mom takes her eyes off of her precious bundle long enough to smile at the hats, and then I get to watch while she puts a pink one on her baby's head. I know that hat.

The papers spill out of the envelope that Carol gave me onto my dining room table and I read each sentence: I can imagine the smile on the person receiving the crocheted items and that puts a smile on my heart; It makes me feel all warm and cozy to think that a sweet preemie baby will be wearing one of my little hats; I knit blankets for babies in hospice care; It makes me happy to know that these soft blankets will comfort dying children.

The words bring tears to my eyes and I have to read them again. Who does that? Who knits for dying children? The world has to know about this. I write an article and a small local paper publishes fourteen thousand copies.

I spend a couple of weeks crocheting a baby blanket and it's all wrapped up and ready to go. The third Wednesday of the month can't come soon enough. I'm a Crafty Lady now.

chapter twenty-four

Home at Last

THE PASSENGER SEAT IS pushed all the way back to accommodate the giant box of donated yarn. I find the shelter, but I'm too early and so nervous that I have to knit for a few minutes to calm myself. I pull two long pink aluminum sticks from the box and cast on with a skein of yellow yarn. Knitting eases me.

These families are homeless and that bothers me a lot. I can't imagine what it must feel like not to have a place to live. There was a time when I might have known (I spent a few days living with my kids in the car) but I had a choice about where to go.

I want to see if knitting will help these kids feel better, happy maybe, give them something to do with their time. It must be terrible in there, living in a home-less shelter.

I walk through the front door with my giant card-board box and everyone is smiling: the man at the front desk, the woman who walks through the lobby, the mother pushing her crying baby in a stroller past me out the front door, two teens in the hallway. This is not what I expected. This must be the front end, where everyone is happy doing their job, so the kids and the trauma must be somewhere else. The director checks me in and points down the hall toward the room where we'll have our first knitting lesson. He gives me directions and I try to pay attention. I meet Casey, the volunteer who watches the kids after dinner, at the door and she welcomes me in.

I smell spaghetti and meatballs and French bread and salad with Italian dressing and I think that I probably should have eaten before I came.

We're having spaghetti for dinner and meatballs. I don't like salad, so I don't eat it. Casey told us that a knitting lady is coming after dinner. I tell my dad to hurry up and eat so I can learn how to knit. I can't leave the cafeteria until my dad finishes. Hurry up, Dad. I've always wanted to knit something...for my whole life I've always wanted to knit.

The first thing I need is a place to plug in my electric pencil sharpener and glue gun, so I ask Casey while she straightens the books on the shelves.

"You can use this one," she points to an outlet on the wall close to the floor, "but you can't leave it there, little kids will be coming soon." Well, this isn't how I planned things. I sit on the floor and sharpen a bunch of dowels and quickly glue wooden beads on the ends but I'm not happy because I wanted the kids to do it.

With beaded dowels sharpened and colored balls of Cascade 220 on the table, I sand a few dowels and set a piece of sandpaper and a pair of needles at each place like party favors. The whole room looks like a giant party; toys, blocks, art and craft supplies, books, crayons, colored dinosaurs, and bins of neon toys that

I don't recognize light up the room. My first knitter walks in.

Embroidered rainbow peace signs adorn the black headband that pulls her long brown hair off of her chubby-cheeked face. Spaghetti sauce stains the corners of her mouth. Her green sweatshirt hoodie is unzipped and a monkey peeks out from a black T-shirt. Her clothes are wrinkled but clean and she smells fresh, like shampoo and fabric softener. We get fifteen stitches cast on.

The table is kidney shaped, like the ones I remember from kindergarten—I find it nearly impossible to get my legs under or squeeze myself into the matching little wooden chair. The girl with the headband is trying to knit while three others rub sandpaper on needles in hopes of discovering the magic of knitting. I get them cast on, but all of the needles aren't working. The wool is sticking on the splintery sticks and the yarn won't slide. I'm sweating and I don't know what to do. I can't fix this right now. I brought aluminum needles, but I wanted the kids to make their own, so they could experience the whole process from the beginning. The homemade needles aren't working and they're waiting for me to show them what to do next.

The girl sitting to my right with the black headband (I think she said her name is Shasta) stretches a long loop from one stick to the other. "I'm so glad you came," she says, as she doesn't look up from her work. "I've been waiting my whole life to knit."

It takes me a second to absorb that.

"How old are you?"

With her needles and a row-and-a-half of knitting poised over the table, she looks at me and says with great pride, "I'm eight."

Other children come in from dinner in the cafeteria and I can't help but notice how young they are. These kids look too young to teach. Casey invites three of the older girls to sit at my little table.

While I pass around sheets of sandpaper, I try to explain the process of smoothing the needles, but the chaos flying around the rest of the room makes my inner self fall apart. Toddlers stack blocks, babies cry, parents drop more kids into Casey's hands, and a volunteer reads a book out loud to anyone who wants to listen. I get each of the girls cast on their almost smooth sticks and find that the girl with the perfectly straight teeth and flawless ebony skin already knows how to knit. Oh, thank God. She can help me with the others having a difficult time grasping the motion of wrapping the yarn around the needles. It doesn't help that the yarn is sticking and I'm on anxiety overload. After a few minutes, I give up on the homemades.

"Here, let's trade those needles for these." I bring up a stack of aluminum needles from the box. "You can take the wooden ones home and sand them smooth for next time, we can try them again next week." I frantically cast on with the too-long shiny needles.

Casey's been out knocking on doors scouting for more interest and brings a strapping young boy to the table. "Can Anthony join?" she asks, and he takes a seat. I have to start over? Are you kidding? Breathe. You can do this.

"Of course, take a seat."

Anthony tips his chair so far back that it rests on its rear legs and he looks as if he might tip over backward. He rights himself and waits for me to tell him what to do.

"You'll have to wait a few minutes until I get everyone else going." He smiles a wide, closed-lipped smile. "Here, sand these." I hand him a pair of sharpened dowels and a piece of sandpaper and show him how to smooth the rough sticks. "Try to smooth down the points a little, too, they're probably too sharp." He gets right to work. The dowels now sanded to his satisfaction, he holds one in each fist, resting the beaded end on the table and the points, like missiles, aim at the ceiling. He looks like he's waiting for something to eat. Meanwhile, the girls bombard me with can-you-fix-this, what-did-I-do-wrong, and what-happened-here questions. My head spins.

"Can I have these?" Anthony picks a ball of red yarn and a pair of red aluminum needles from the table, and I shake my head yes while I help the girl next to me with her dropped stitch.

Anthony watches and waits for something to happen and never says another word. I glance his way and offer a look of "I'm sorry," which he seems to understand. When he leaves, I promise to teach him next week, and tell him that he'll be first in line. He shows his mom and dad his yarn and sticks when they appear in the doorway. They pat him on the back and shoot me a very nice thank you smile. I've never seen more patient children anywhere. I wish I had their patience, or calm, or whatever it is.

Before I leave, I ask Casey if we could have a room with a table—they said we would have a room, and I was having a hard time teaching with all the commotion and small children wanting to play with the sharp sticks and colored balls.

"I don't think I can sit in these chairs again." I muster a tight grimace. She takes me to a room next door with L-shaped couches, a television, and a few chairs. "No table? I really need a table, do you have a table and some folding chairs?" I think I might be able to borrow a folding table and chairs, but I don't know if they would fit in my car.

"I'll try to find some." Now I feel better. I leave with a hope for an easier time next week. I'll get them real needles...nice bamboo needles from home, and bring more yarn. They like the bright colors and the variegated yarn.

I'm looking forward to seeing the kids this week, I'm actually excited, and I don't get lost until I try to navigate the facility. Where was that room? I should have asked at the front desk. There it is, but the door is locked. Now what? A teenager in the hallway tells me that everyone is still eating dinner and she can show me where the cafeteria is. I drop my box and follow her down a maze of colored walls. "Is Casey there?" She says yes. This week I smell beef stew or something meaty. I think how nice it must be to have food served to you every day. Casey gets up when she sees me, says hello, and walks me back to the room to unlock the door. She opens the door to the room with the couches.

"No table?" I ask. I was expecting a folding table.

"Oh, we have this one, but the chairs are...I'll show you." She opens a storage closet and a mound of things block a few folding chairs that I can only see the tops of. I can tell by the look on her face that she doesn't really want to dig through the pile to get me a few chairs.

"Never mind, we can use the little chairs from the kids room." My hips hurt at the thought. "Or they can sit on the couches. That might work."

"Are you sure?" She looks tired. While we move a

small rollout table from against the wall, she tells me that she volunteers here every day after her college classes. I marvel at how she can go to school, take care of all these kids, and have time to get her homework done.

"It's a challenge," she says, "but I love what I do."

I see two regular-sized chairs in the room, so I'll be okay. I set them around the table and place a bunch of colored balls and needles out, so it'll look like a big pile of fun when the kids come.

Anthony arrives first, carrying his red needles and a now-tangled ball of red yarn. He sits in the only other adult-sized chair at the head of the table.

"Anthony...dude," I say. His eyes light up today and his smile is contagious. "Ready to learn?" He shakes his head without a word.

I trade him his tangled yarn for a new ball and offer him a pair of bamboo needles, but he wants to keep the cool red aluminum ones that I gave him last week. No worries, they'll work fine. While I cast on twenty stitches and knit two rows, a mom and her daughter peek into the room.

"Are you the Knitting Lady?"

I like the sound of that. "I am, come on in...pick a ball of yarn and a pair of needles and let's get you knitting." I get big smiles from both of them. Shasta is not with them. I never asked everyone's names and I was so nervous that I didn't tell them mine.

I think I'll just be the Knitting Lady.

Our room is small, but my dad and I fit in here just fine. It's better than sleeping in the car...or on the street. I don't want to talk about it. We had pizza for dinner tonight, pepperoni and cheese pizza. I have a box that I keep my

*yarn in, because my aunt gave me some yarn a long time
ago and I still have it. The knitting lady gave me three
balls...a purple and a blue and a dark purple. I like the way
she wraps her arms around me when she moves my hands
and makes them knit. I need help so I can remember what
to do next. I tried it by myself but I messed it all up. Is
somebody at the door?*

*"Who is it? Oh, hi Casey. Oh, knitting again? I almost
forgot! Dad, I'm going to knitting. Wait...I need my box.
Bye!"*

There she is, I was hoping she would come. No headband
today. She's wearing a woven hat in pinks and purples
and when she sits down, I tell her I like her hat and ask
her what her name is.

"It's Shasta, don't you remember?"

Three girls, a mom, and Anthony are knitting away
with minimal fuss. I'm surprised at how quickly they're
picking it up this week (must be the needles, I think), and
I tell them what a good job they're doing. I concentrate
on helping the kids knit and the bits of chaos filtering
in from the other room are much more manageable. I'm
having fun.

"I brought my knitting," Shasta says, as she opens her
painted cardboard box. Inside are a set of circle looms,
the three balls of Cascade 220, and some tangled yarn
that smells mildly of mothballs. Several sets of needles,
including the hand-sanded homemade ones, poke out
over the sides of the box.

"I was hoping you'd come because I need help with
this." She digs in her box and delicately places a neon-
green circular loom on the table. Anthony stops knitting
to see what it is. The mother-and-daughter team are deep

in conversation about how pretty all the colors are, and what do you want to make, and isn't this fun.

"I really don't know how to use one of those things," I say, as difficult as it is to admit the truth. "But I can try. I think it works like the spool with the nails that my brother and I played with."

"You do it like this." Shasta wraps blue yarn around the perimeter of the loom once then around each individual peg and, after fishing a bent stick from her box, she flips a loop over and off the peg. "See? I can do it, but I don't know how to finish it. I want to make a hat, like the one I'm wearing. My aunt made this for me." She stops looping and pats her head. I lean over to get a closer look, to see how it's knitted.

"It's beautiful." We all agree.

Casey comes in and tells me that they need the room for reading time. I guess she sees my disappointment, as it feels like we just got started.

"Sorry, seven thirty is reading time."

"No worries, I'll be back and we'll do it again next week. You guys take all the yarn you want, and practice until I see you next week, okay?"

"We can have more?"

"It's all for you guys, people from all over sent this yarn just for you."

I stay and clean up around the table. On the way out the front door, I see the mom and her daughter knitting together on a couch in the front lobby.

"We didn't want to stop knitting," the mom says. They wave at me and smile and I know I'm here for a reason.

The next week something comes up and I don't go to the shelter.

Where is the knitting lady? I need to ask her a question. She said she would come on Wednesday and it's Wednesday. She said she'd be here after dinner and it's after dinner and she's not here.

"Where were you? You said you'd be here, I was looking for you, we thought you were never coming back." Shasta has her peace-sign headband on and she and two others are waiting in the hallway. I feel like I'm being scolded. Guilt times three.

"I'm really sorry I couldn't come. Let's see what you have going."

Casey opens the door and I put another box of yarn on the table. The mom and daughter and two new kids show up...a brother and a sister. I cast on for them and show them how to knit. Every week we start over. They get a new pair of needles and a new ball of yarn and a new cast-on and another lesson. It's slow going, and I worry that if we don't get further along, they might lose interest. I really want them to get to the point where they can hold up a piece of knitting and feel the accomplishment. And then I remember that they're trying something new, and that every stitch, no matter how it turns out, is a huge accomplishment.

Brother makes a few stitches and then decides to find a truck to play with in the other room, but little sister stays to knit. I let the girls take turns with my camera and they capture the fun. Casey sees the camera and takes me aside to tell me that some of the children don't have photo releases, and I can't use their pictures. "If a picture gets out of those two, the father will know where they are."

It never occurred to me that this is a safe haven for

families in trouble. Things are starting to make sense. It's a good thing they have this place.

"How long are you going to stay?" Shasta asks.

"Until reading time, we have to leave at seven thirty."

"No, I mean for knitting. Will you be here until June? We're leaving in June. We got a house and we're moving in June. You wanna know the best part about a house?"

"What's the best part about a house?"

"The bathroom. Our new house has a bathroom inside the house. A girl needs a bathroom." I laugh out loud and she does, too. The whole room giggles, except for smiling Anthony. His cheeks are the color of his yarn.

A mother strolls in with a three-year-old. "What are you guys doing in here?"

"We're knitting, come on in."

"I used to knit," she says, "in another lifetime." She sits on the couch next to another mom, and her three-year-old starts a major tantrum. I hand the mom a set of needles with a few rows already knit and wait for her to try. She makes a perfect knitted stitch.

"See? It's like riding a bike, as soon as you touch it, you remember." I pat her on the back and sit back down at the table with the kids. I watch her knit as her toddler's meltdown intensifies. He throws his head back and screams louder and stomps his feet, but his mother is intent on knitting.

"Just wait, one more stitch. Wait a minute, let me finish this row." She is determined. A minute of knitting nirvana in the midst of a meltdown is a relief. I see it on her face and it's hard not to laugh because I know exactly how she feels.

On the way to my car, I run into the young girl and her mother, the two who helped each other knit, the ones who sat together knitting on the couch in the front entry, the two with the biggest smiles.

"I'll see you next week," I call out as I open the car door.

"We won't be here, we won't be coming back," the mother says. "We're moving."

"You're moving? Where are you going?" Disappointment washes through me. We just found each other. I didn't teach you enough. You can't leave yet. And then it hits me. They're moving...to a house...away from the homeless shelter...so as not to be homeless. They don't have enough yarn.

"Wait. Take some more yarn with you. Here, take it all, do you have room?" I hand her the box. The mother tips the box toward the light of the streetlamp and she and her daughter beam as they sift through it. It's tearing me up that they're leaving, and then I see the joy on their faces and I smile through my tears.

chapter twenty-five

Boot Camp

I'M SO EXCITED BECAUSE our oldest member, Dorothy, is coming to knitting group today. Her grandson is stationed in Afghanistan and she's been knitting helmet liners to send to the men and women in his platoon. Unbeknownst to her, the store offered a free pattern and a discount on a ball of Cascade Superwash yarn to anyone who wanted to make one, and the yarn shop staff (which includes me) and a bunch of our customers have been secretly knitting the liners for weeks. I've been collecting them and stashing them in bags under the counter just waiting for today, because tomorrow, she told us, is the day she would be mailing her knitted love to keep her grandson and his buddies warm.

I laid out ninety-seven helmet liners in all shades of army greens and browns and grays and we waited for Dorothy to show up. When she did, she burst into tears. "I'm not going to stop crying," she told us. She hugged every one of us at the table. She was so taken that she couldn't stay and knit. We packed the liners into brown paper bags and Dorothy carried them out in both arms, leaving us all in tears.

"Wow, that was awesome," I say. "I can't imagine how hard it must be to be over there fighting for us, and how special it would be to get a package from home like that. I wish I could see her grandson's face."

Just as Dorothy leaves, Becky, our newest member, walks into the room and sits down.

I met Becky when she came into the store to buy some yarn. She bought two hanks of Debbie Bliss Rialto Lace and when I offered to wind it into balls for her, she thanked me profusely. Two times four-hundred-twenty-six-and-a-half yards is all my wrist can take in one sitting, but I like to wind yarn because it makes the swift look like a sideways Ferris wheel. Becky stood with me and waited while I cranked the ball winder, and when I ask, she says that her father taught her to knit.

"Really?" My eyebrows ride up under my bangs.

"It was sometime in the sixties; I think I was in first grade. I saw a little 'How to Knit' kit in a craft store that came with a book and a pair of little needles and some red yarn. I really wanted it, but I didn't know if anybody would be able to help me, because I was left-handed and dyslexic and no one in my family knit. My father, with his Navy background tying knots and all, taught me how to macramé. Dad was left-handed too. When he was in school the nuns made everyone write right-handed so he knew how to use both hands. My dad was wonderful. He taught himself how to knit from that little book and then he taught me."

My arm is starting to ache, but I have another skein to wind. Becky offers to wind some, but I don't want to relinquish control. "I'm having fun. I really don't mind; I like it. Do you remember what you made back then?"

"I made ponchos out of small little squares for my

dolls...I think I still have my first little pink square blanket that I knit for my Barbie. I kept at it and eventually got good enough to do some teaching for my daughter's Girl Scout troop. I helped them make simple squares and we sewed them together and donated them to the needy. I wanted them to know that knitting is a great learning tool, and how it allows you to give of yourself. Making something for someone else, what can be better for the soul than that?"

"Not a thing. So what are you making with this gorgeous yarn?" We always ask each other the same questions...knitters just want to know.

"Right now I'm involved in a church prayer shawl group. We pray over each stitch, hoping to give comfort and warmth and hugs to someone who needs it. Growing up a Catholic, there was always the rosary to be said. Say a prayer, move a bead. Such a peace comes over us while we pray, giving thanks and asking our petitions. Knit, purl, turn a row; repetition is a lot like prayers. When my son went off to boot camp last year, knitting gave my hands something to do, my mind something to focus on—turn your thoughts over to God and see how he can help you take one long piece of thread and create a beautiful piece of artwork—it was a total release for all of my stress and worries. When I finish this shawl, I'm starting a new project to donate to a fundraiser for our military."

I finish winding two perfectly beautiful lace balls and package them up at the register and then I invite Becky to join our knitting group that meets in the store in a few days.

"I would love to come," she says, "but I might be a little late."

"No worries, just come whenever."

"Sorry I'm late," Becky says. "What did I miss?"

No one in the group is smiling. Wads of tissues litter the table.

"What's going on?" Becky looks to me and I tell her what just happened with Dorothy and the helmet liners and her grandson in Afghanistan.

"You did that for our boys over there? That's wonderful. I pray for them every day."

I introduce Becky to the group. Everyone marvels at the beginnings of her shawl and she tells them the same story we shared a few days ago. She has such an uplifting spirit.

It's three weeks later and Dorothy comes to knitting group with a package and a grin from ear to ear. She looks like a little kid, even at eighty-something, with some exciting news that she can't wait to tell us.

"What is it, Dorothy?"

"Look what I got today!" She takes an eight-by-ten glossy out of a manila envelope and races around the table. No one can believe it. An entire platoon, dressed in gray and white fatigues, is holding their helmets crooked in their arms and every face is smiling under green and brown and gray helmet liners.

"That's him...that's my grandson!" Dorothy's pride spills over everything.

"There were so many, he said. There were so many that they shared the rest with all the other platoons."

part nine
Ending

chapter twenty-six

Cherry Street

PAINFUL LIFE EVENTS HAPPEN in rapid succession, too many for me to know what to do. Daytimes turn into long hours of waiting for darkness and sleep to release me from my agony. Depression consumes me. Old behaviors lie just within my reach and I drink again for relief that I hope to find. Instead, I am sick and poisoned and I riddle myself with guilt. I need help again. After thirty years, I never imagined that I would be unstable enough to seek the advice of a therapist.

I pick her name from a list. *Dr. Larimore...for depression, anxiety, and phase of life issues.* Yes, that sounds exactly right because that's what I have. When I call the number, I like the sound of her voice on the recorded message. I make an appointment and it takes me an hour to decide which knitting project to bring. I haven't worked on any of them in weeks.

The small blue Victorian house sits close to its neighbors on a secluded street, edged with fully grown trees in one of the oldest parts of town. Cracked and worn with time, the sidewalk surrounds a finely manicured lawn, which, unlike mine, contains no weeds. Painted steps lead the way to a porch at the front door where I stand and wonder if I really need to be here. My heart feels heavy with failure.

Tap-tap-tap. I rap lightly on the door. This doesn't look like a doctor's office. The number above the door matches the one on the crumpled paper I left in the car and this is Cherry Street so I must be in the right place. I try again. Tap-tap-tap and the door opens inward.

Bent forward with one hand on the doorknob and the other covering her mouth while trying to swallow, she seems somewhat surprised and caught off guard. For a second I think I might have interrupted someone's lunch. She doesn't look like a doctor.

"Oh...come in." Still covering her mouth, she motions with her free hand after a quick glance at her watch. "I have an appointment," I say with slight confidence, and follow her to a living room, no, a waiting room, I see. This old house has been converted into offices. Relieved that I'm in the right place, the tightness in my chest eases slightly but I still have a death grip on my knitting bag.

"You're a little early." She smiles at me, having finally swallowed. "Have a seat and I'll be back out in a few minutes." I'm always early. I have my knitting.

I survey my choices in the nicely decorated room, glad to be alone. The black leather sofa appears too cushy and faces the wall, not a position I like to be in, so I choose the matching leather chair facing it and sit down on the edge.

I want to knit, but I need to get comfortable. I look over the neatly stacked rows of magazines on the gigantic glass-topped coffee table but nothing interests me. What is that white noise, I wonder. Soothing and mysteriously hidden, I think it clever for a therapist to have whatever it is gurgling throughout the waiting room. I really need to knit.

Drawn to the sun streaming through the windows in the west corner of the room, I pick up my bag and move to a more inviting reception room chair. Not happy with the location, I push the chair into the corner next to a tall, well-watered corn plant. Hoping not to get in trouble, I ease the slatted wooden shutters open all the way so the sun will shine directly on my always cold fingers. This is a perfect spot for knitting. With the wool in my hands and the chart on my knee, I soon drift to the comfort place and, oblivious to time, let it consume me.

Just as I get into the rhythm of my two-handed stranded Fair Isle scarf pattern—three greens, one blue, one green, three blues—Dr. Larimore appears in the hallway. I finish a few stitches while she watches and then drop it into my bag and stand up.

"Your knitting is beautiful," she says as I follow her. "What are you making?"

"Oh, just a mindless scarf, nothing special, thanks." We've broken the ice. I like her.

I am struck by the comfort in her office. The same kind of black leather sofa faces a large window behind the chair where she sits. One wall is covered with white shelves containing hundreds of little figures and toys—everything from alligators and army men to airplanes and trains. I ask about the wall of toys and she explains that this was the office of another doctor who used these things for sand tray therapy.

"I would love to do that," I say, knowing that we probably won't. I wonder what moving things around in a sandbox says about a person. I put my knitting bag next to my feet and take a seat on the comfortable leather couch and wait for the usual intake questions. I don't want to start at the beginning. I want her to help me with the me that's here now, to keep me from becoming the old me from before.

"How can I help you?" She then asks all the right questions. I tell her that I'm having fear of success issues, my confidence in myself is shattered, that I was sober for twenty-two years but self-medicated with alcohol when something bad happened that I thought was my fault, and I'm afraid of everything that might propel me in a forward direction.

"My father told me that I would never amount to anything," I say, "and I lived my life as if he was right, and now I know it's not true, but I keep falling down and I need a new set of tools. I don't know how to process things." I reach down and pull my knitting from its bag to the couch. I want it close to me, where I can touch it.

"Tell me about your knitting," she says.

"Well, I'm worried about that, too." I scoop up the ball of yarn attached to my scarf. "I stopped knitting. I usually knit every day. Oh, I'm knitting a little here and there, like today in the waiting room, but not like usual. Knitting is who I am, knitting is what makes me happy."

She takes notes in a black leather binder while she sits straight, shoulders back, and responds to my comments. Unusual, I think. Most therapists ask, "And how does that make you feel?" and then all I do is cry. This one talks to me.

"I lost a lot of weight lately, not in the healthy way. I ended up in the hospital with a knot in my stomach the size of a rock and they told me it was stress." I tell her how much I used to weigh, and what I weigh now, so she'll know how sick I am.

I don't tell her my secret. And then our time is up. I hate it when the time is up. I write a check and we make an appointment for next week.

This week I bring my camera. I take pictures of everything: the converted house, the street sign, the front lawn, the waiting room, the view from the window, and the pictures on the wall. I take a picture of a picture of fat sheep hanging on the wall in the bathroom. If I take pictures then I'll remember. I wait in my seat in the corner and take out the same piece of knitting that I haven't touched since the last visit and before I get a chance to work on it, Dr. Larimore invites me into her office. I'm feeling a little uneasy today, as if I know stuff is going to come up. It always does, maybe that's what I'm afraid of. I want to tell the truth, so she can help me.

"I've been keeping things bottled up," I say, and then the floodgates open. I tell her about my second cousin, how we found each other after forty years, and how we were in love as young teenagers and how for the last three months, I've spent every waking minute talking to him on the computer. I tell her that it was unhealthy, the things we talked about, imagining that we could turn back time and run away together. I wanted the constant communication and innuendos to stop, but I didn't know how.

"One day, I posted something, and he got mad. He called me stupid and yelled at me. He screamed a whole message in capital letters. He might as well have punched me in the face. The only person who ever understood me as a child and knew my situation at home crushed me. I sent him a message that I wasn't going to be yelled at, not even on the computer. We stopped talking. I was relieved, in a way, because now I could get back to knitting and spending time with my family."

Dr. Larimore is writing in her book and I'm soaking through a box of tissues.

"Three days later I snuck a look at his Facebook page, just to see what he was up to...and there was a message there, on his page...about how sad...about how much he would be missed..."

She sits quietly and waits while I cry.

"He died. He dropped dead of a heart attack. It happened right after I told him that we were finished. I know, because I looked at the time the message was posted. I felt like I had something to do with it. I thought he died because he was mad at me. I know it's not true, but I was traumatized for weeks. I drank over it. I still wonder."

I can tell by her shift in posture that our time is up again. I pick up my purse to write a check and my knitting tumbles out of its bag. I pick it up carefully and put it back.

"I have something I want you to do," she says, as she closes her binder. "I want you to knit at least two hours a day. Every day for at least two hours. That's my recommendation."

I go home and I start to knit. It happens that a friend calls me and asks me to design something with her hand-dyed yarn. Isn't that always the way? She sends me a box full of the softest, most beautiful yarn that I've ever seen. I dive in. I knit like I used to, happy to be doing what I love. I spend more than the recommended two hours every day and create pattern after pattern. I feel like myself again, less fearful and more confident. I look forward to getting up every day so I can work on my patterns in the early morning light. Once again, my pieces hang in a yarn shop. The patterns are for sale right now. Dr. Larimore was right. I had the tools all along.

On our last visit she tells me that it's lovely to see me so relaxed. During our session, she doesn't write anything down in her notebook. I know our time is up.

On the way out the door, I offer to teach her to knit. She says she'll think about it.

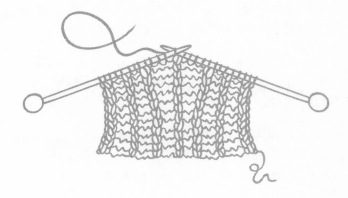

chapter twenty-seven

The Gift

MY LAST CLEAR RECOLLECTION is me standing in his doorway.

I am stuck with fear, but the choice to enter has already been made. My father calls to me from his bed and, in his steely blue eyes, I see a warmth and light that I don't recall, and then I remember that he is my daddy and I sit on the edge of his bed.

I'm surprised at his withering. His once six-foot-six frame looks to be much smaller, and the protrusions from under the sheet are bonelike where there was once a man of flesh.

"Hi Dad." I muster all of the happiness that I can find for him. My heart is broken, not because he is dying, but because I am still hurt and unforgiving.

His sunken eyes disturb me while I look at his face from where I sit, and we talk about boredom and what books he has read.

My sister is with me and she sits in the small chair under the window on the north side; this is the first time in forty years that the three of us have been together in the same room. After a silence the size of outer space,

I recall a photograph and bring up its memory.

"Remember the time we went to see the deer and we had a picnic there?" I try hard to recall anything else that will make him happy, but I am at a loss. And then I see the antique wooden swift.

"Oh, Dad, I want that."

"Do you know what that is?"

Of course I do, but how would he know that? I'm not really sure if he remembers that I knit. "It looks like a spinning wheel, but it's not. It's the thing that winds the yarn into a ball."

"Do you like it?" His eyes brighten.

"I love it, Dad."

"Then you can have it, I'll have it shipped to your house."

"Really?" I'm a little girl again and I am happy because I got what I wanted.

My sister stirs from her silence, and I'm grateful because I don't know what else to say.

I don't remember to tell him how loved I felt sometimes when, after lowering the Sunday paper, he would pat-pat the couch and invite me to climb up and sit next to him and he would let me rest my head on his chest and I would listen to the th-thump of his heart and then he would stroke my hair once or twice before lifting his paper to the light.

"Are you hungry, Dad?" my sister asks him. "What would you like for lunch?"

I've flown a long way to get here and I'm hungry but I don't know if I can eat. Seeing my father in his weakened state has left me with a knot that food probably won't fix.

"Remember the liverwurst sandwiches we used to

have? Yeah, with mayonnaise on white bread, and sometimes I would put green relish on it, remember?" I ask them both.

"I haven't had a liverwurst sandwich in years. I love liverwurst." His voice sounds tired.

"Me, too," my sister says. She drives to the store for the makings and leaves me alone with my father.

I rub the back of my fingers softly against his freshly shaven cheek while I examine the horseshoe scar that still covers the top of his head. I remember the green wool vest turned crimson with his dried blood, and think what a good thing it was that he was drunk that night when he drove into that tree and sheared the top of his head off as he was catapulted through the windshield. I sit a little closer to him, like my mother did for days, when she tweezed shards of glass from his head and plinked them into an ashtray. I move my hand from his cheek and trace the scar with my finger.

"You don't have much hair left, Dad." His smile reveals spittle at the corners of his mouth, and I see amusement in his eyes.

"Do you want to see what I brought?" I reach into the bag at the side of the bed. "Look, it's a bear. I made it."

With a strand of wool and a strand of mohair held together, I painstakingly followed a row-by-row pattern, and then I stuffed the toy with a plastic bag and felted it. After it dried, I stuffed it again with fiberfill and then stitched up his back end perfectly. His little ears sat in just the right spot, but it took days to get up the confidence to embroider his face. The face was the hardest part...if you don't get the face just right, it just looks wrong. My confidence wavered every time I threaded the needle with black floss, but after a few tries, I knew

I got it right because the look on the bear's face makes me happy...it brings him to life and I smile every time I look at him.

Never in my life have I seen anything resembling the fascination that I see on my father's face. He turns the fuzzy cream-colored bear over and over, petting its high haunches, examining each foot with its soft pad and five toes.

"I like this," he says. "I really like this...because it looks like a National Geographic bear, not a toy, not a toy like other bears. It looks like a real bear."

I'm beaming.

"You made this for me?"

His question surprises me. I didn't. I brought it to show him what I love to do, and how good I am at it. I brought it to show him a piece of my success. I brought it to show him that he was wrong.

"Of course, Dad, I made it for you." He is suddenly childlike, grinning and amused with his gift. How different he is from the father who frightened me with his loud obscenities, smashing of furniture, and drunken rages. How playful he seems against the image I carry of him pressing a butcher knife to my mother's throat. He brings the bear closer and looks into its face.

My stepmother and my sister enter the room with a plate full of sandwiches and he shows off his knitted prize. After much adoration, Tina, my stepmother, places the bear—per my father's instructions—on the small television across the room under the picture of his beloved cat Marv.

"Why, that bear looks as though he might want to jump right off of that TV and into my lap," he says. I have never seen him so silly.

"Could you make more?" he asks. "My nieces would love one of these."

"How many do you need?" Some of the special we've just shared goes away as I imagine myself making two more bears for children that I don't know. And then I see the joy on my father's face and I tell him that I would love to knit more for his nieces.

I tell my father not to be afraid, and then I tell him about the time I took too many pills by accident and died, and I tell him how wonderful it was and please don't be afraid to go.

I don't remember what we talk about while we eat. I think that my sister looks too thin, and then my father finishes a whole sandwich. Something, he says, he hasn't done in a year.

Three months later, the pouch connected to the seat in front of me on the airplane is filled with tissues. I can't peel my forehead off of the window that looks out to the rest of the world, nor clamp the flow of tears.

My knitting sits untouched in my carry-on and my head hurts because I have cried too long. Not because my father is gone, but because I am still blaming and unforgiving and I don't know how to fix that.

It is a damp and misty New England morning. A man wearing a plaid kilt and cabled socks plays his bagpipes under the canopy of a sassafras tree while family members that I have not seen in forever stand next to one another in a semicircle. I am holding onto the arm of my father's brother, and I lean into his chest and tell him that I always wished he was my father; he squeezes my arm and whispers that he knows, and that he loves me, too.

Tina asks if anyone has something to say and I am

surprised at her composure. My sister turns to me with a pleading look, but I'm not prepared for the question. Although I want to be strong, I fall apart as I thank Tina for loving him.

The time has come to take him where he asked to be scattered and my sister and I wait for the boat on a large rock next to the dock. A sunny breeze blows my hair off of my face.

The charter boat is grand, and while we ride the swells of waves, I feel as though I'm on a ride at the fair, and for a minute I forget why we're here. As we travel around the point, I see the shoreline and the beaches where I spent my childhood, and then, through the woods at the top of the hill, there it is—the house my father built.

Tina signals to the captain and the boat chugs and slows. This is the place. I wait for instruction, as I have never done this before. Tina tosses rose petals from their garden overboard from a large brown paper bag and, after she opens a small plastic bag, hands me his ashes.

"Go ahead, you dump some and then we'll dump some."

This is creepy. When I tilt the small plastic bag, the wind kicks some of the contents back into my face, and I am stunned while Tina laughs.

"He would have laughed at that, too." She smiles at me.

We leave a long trail of rose petals in our wake as we return to the docks.

My father was a hard and bitter man. He told me once that I would never amount to anything and I believed him, as I was a child and he was my father. Hurt, resentful, and defiant, I would spend a lifetime fighting to prove him wrong.

The gift of the bear brought a spark of selfless-ness, something unfamiliar to me. To see such joy that my accomplishment brought him was a turning point, although it would take many years before I understood the significance of it all. It would be during those years, while in the comfort of knitting, that my world would open to a place where questions revealed answers and I received the biggest gift of all.

chapter twenty-eight

Full Circle

FROM A DISTANCE, a prism of light fractures her once jet-black hair into a thousand strands of silver frost. Exhausted from nerves and a twelve-hour journey, I drop my bags and hug my mother.

Her sister drives us from the tiny airport and my mother sits next to me in the backseat with her hand resting on mine, and then she strokes my hair and tells me how beautiful I am. Although I live three thousand miles away and it's been four years since our last visit, the smell of the New England summer night air makes me feel as though I never left home. She closes the door to the guest room and I inhale the pillow and comforter and I am asleep.

Daylight brings blue skies and puffy clouds—the kind of day that reminds me of the smell of fresh sheets and crispy towels blowing in an easy breeze on a cotton clothesline. From my seat at the dining room table, crystal rays shimmer off the pool, and while I imagine a much-loved horse living in the small red barn with white trim, a chipmunk scampers across the deck. Humming-birds battle for red nectar just inches from the bay window. It's lovely here.

Mother pours boiling water into a cup of dark crystals and sits in her place at the table, and when she sits, I feel sadness because the love of her life, her second husband is no longer in his place across from her. As if she reads my mind, she says that she misses him terribly. I can't imagine how that feels because I still have my love at home.

She absentmindedly pencils in a few numbers on her Sudoku puzzle and when she looks up, she rests her chin in her hands with her elbows on the table and beams her face into a smile as big as the moon. I swallow a mouthful of coffee and I want to tell her so many things.

I want to tell her that I paid attention when she told me that eyeballs wiggle under their lids if you pretend to be asleep, and that I practiced keeping my eyes very still. I want to tell her how good I was at not wiggling my eyeballs the afternoon my father came into my room and aimed a gun at my head while he stood at the foot of my bed.

I want to tell her that it was me who stole the cough drops, so we can finally close that chapter.

I want to tell her that I'm sorry I was outside the front door that night with bare feet in the snow and I especially want to say I'm sorry for picking up the razor blade the next day and using it on myself.

I want to tell her I feel awful because I didn't tell on the neighbor down the street when he raped me and Maryellen, because I might have saved the children who followed. I want to tell her about the time I took too many pills and died, and how I gave up on myself the night I lay down in the middle of the street at four o'clock in the morning and how scared I was when the tires screeched on the wet pavement and stopped inches from the back of my head.

I want to tell her about the fire that I set in the field the night before I got rescued by Carol and Shawnee, and I want to tell her that I'm sorry I was mad because I thought she never loved me. Most of all, I want to thank her for knitting.

"Well, darling, show me what you're working on." She glances toward my knitting bag, her face still beaming.

"Well, I have this scarf that I've been knitting in the airport and on the plane. It's Noro yarn." I plop a length of colorful Cheshire cat stripes onto the table, followed by two tangled balls of soft blue and pink and purple cotton. "It's made with two different skeins and you work three rows with one ball, then three rows with the second. You carry the yarn up the sides so you don't have to tuck in any ends, see?" She examines the edge. "It's a mindless knit one purl one, so it looks the same on both sides."

"This is beautiful, honey. The colors are gorgeous."

"That's the Noro, the colors all come in one ball. It's not my pattern, Jared Flood designed it—his stuff is all over the Internet. Brooklyn Tweed, don't you love that name for a yarn company? He's a photographer, too." I wrap the scarf around my neck while I fish around in my bag. "Here's one of my designs that I'm working on." I pull out the back and a half-finished front to a black and gray chevron patterned jacket. "I'm making this with Knit Picks yarn and then they'll sell the pattern at their site."

"I don't know how you come up with all of these ideas." She sips her coffee and pencils in another number into her puzzle and then erases it.

"I wish I knew how to play that game." I like math. I get a brief lesson on the rules of Sudoku.

"I still do my crossword puzzles, but I like this better," she says.

"Do you want to see what else I brought?"

"Of course, I would love to see…more coffee?"

"Sure, Mom, thanks." She puts the kettle on the stove.

I open my notebook to a sketch that I've colored in with colored pencils.

"This is how I design my patterns. I find something I like, like this one from a catalog." The torn paper drops to the floor. "Oops, then I trace the outline of the model because I can't draw people, and then I design the jacket. Then comes the fun part."

"I don't know how you find the energy to accomplish all that you do with your knitting and your designs." The kettle whistles and I snap her picture while she stands in front of the kitchen window. Neither of us likes to have our picture taken and when I catch her off guard, she grimaces. She grimaces again when she sees her reflection in the camera.

"Too bad, Ma. I want a picture of you."

I go on to explain how I draw out a picture for each size, knit a gauge swatch, and then plug in the numbers. "I write the pattern first and then I knit it to see if the numbers are right. It's like solving a math puzzle." She beams her "I love you" smile again.

"I'm amazed at what you do."

"Thanks, Mom."

The pool shimmers in the morning sun and, as though she reads my mind, asks if I want to see the yard. I leave my scarf on the table and follow her through the sunroom out onto the deck. Red, pink, and magenta azaleas are in full bloom. Bright blue morning glories twine around the pump-house door and bunches of dainty white flowers poke through river rock at the far side of the pool. Tomatoes ripen in pots on the stone patio next to the compost pile. Pinned with wooden pins, a towel hangs from the umbrella clothesline at the side of the house. Suddenly, I smell sheets and crunchy upside-down clothes. What a beautiful day.

"They're going crazy this year, these azaleas." She looks into the birdbath for a frog who, she says, has taken up residence in the pool. "I come out here in the mornings and usually find him on the boat."

"The boat?" We walk around to the far side of the pool and I see a plastic boat dragging a small net.

"It's a leaf catcher—or a ride for frogs." She laughs. "They come out at night and jump into the pool. This is the only thing that saves them. I lose a few every year." Poor frogs. "You must be starving."

I know my mother feels like she has to entertain me, and this makes her uncomfortable, so I explain while we meander back to the house that I don't eat much and we can go to the store whenever she wants.

"Well..." she seems anxious. "All I have is a few tomatoes and some fruit...and bread. I have bread." She rifles through the cupboard.

"Mom, I would love a tomato sandwich, it's my favorite." I'm serious. Garden-ripe tomatoes, salt, pepper, mayonnaise, and white bread, it doesn't get much better. She opens the cellar door to the pantry.

"I have pickled beets."

"I love pickled beets. I remember you used to eat them out of the can over the kitchen sink...and ketchup and sugar on bread...and cold baked beans and canned green beans."

"I still do." No wonder we have the same taste, except for the ketchup and sugar. No wonder I think of her every time I open a can of beans.

After lunch we snooze in the sunroom and read. I knit while Boston beats the Yankees.

We finish off the evening watching a rodeo show on TV with cowboys riding bulls. Really, Mom, bull riding?

After a night of peaceful sleep, I find my mother in the morning already at her place at the dining table and an empty coffee cup waiting for me on the counter.

"Good morning, darling, did you sleep well?"

"Morning, Mom." I massage her shoulders while I glance at her Sudoku puzzle. "I slept like a log."

After coffee, we take a short drive to the farmer's market to stock up on fruit and veggies for the week. The first thing I see as we walk up the hill is a lady knitting a pair of socks under a tree in the shade. We talk about yarns and socks and knitting. Mom pauses halfway up the hill to catch her breath. Shoot, I forgot about the emphysema.

"Are you okay, Mom?" I walk down to where she's bent over with her hands on her knees.

"I'm fine. Just have to rest a minute." I think that this might be too much for her but she won't admit that she's struggling. I take her arm and we bag a few tomatoes, peaches, strawberries, string beans, and a dozen ears of sweet corn on the cob.

On the way home, clouds darken and cross in front of the sun. They bring thunder and lightning and dump a warm summer rain. We hurry inside, put a pot on for the corn, and watch the rain pelt the pool.

"Remember when we were young and we would run around in the pouring rain? We would have to scramble to pull all of the clothes in from the clothesline before they got soaked. I loved playing in between the sheets; you remember the clothesline? We had the biggest clothesline of anyone I ever knew."

She holds an ear of corn in midair and looks at me. Something in her eyes isn't right. "Your father tied me up with that clothesline, you know."

In that instant, time stands still. In the movie behind my eyes, all the bad parts of my childhood begin to make sense. Of course she couldn't rescue me.

And then she tells me more truth. For seven days.

I ask questions. I get answers. No tears, no emotional meltdown, just a mother and a daughter sharing truths together.

"This is how it should have been when I was growing up, Mom."

"I know," she says. Her guilt hurts my heart.

"Tell me what happened to him, Mom. What happened in his life that made him the way he was?"

"It might have been that when he was a kid, he fell out of a third-story window and landed on his head."

"Is that how he got that dent in his head?" I smile at her. "He told us he got kicked by a horse."

We check in at the tiny gray airport and we sit in gray plastic chairs and we wait. Saying good-bye is harder this time because we are changed and she is the mother I always wanted. The announcement to board the plane comes over the intercom and I don't want to cry, but I feel tears and I try to blink them away.

I pick up my knitting bag and she walks me to the gate. "Thanks for telling me everything, Mom."

"You know," she says, "I'm happy for you that you're writing all of your memories, but I really don't remember much of those twelve years that I was married to him."

What? All twelve years? My entire childhood? If you don't remember, then you can't know what I went through. And then, just as quickly as the thoughts come, they disappear.

"That's great, Mom, I'm glad you don't have to carry that garbage around with you anymore." I hug her as tight as her body will allow, and her face beams me a smile as big as the moon.

"I love you, Mom."

Through the comfort of knitting, of shared stories, of friendships and giving, my lost and confused mind is able to sort things out and I find what I've been searching for.

I find my soul.

I forgive my father. I feel my mother's love. Finally, I'm able to reach deep down inside myself and hug the little girl who lives there and pull myself up from the center, much in the same way you start a new ball of yarn.

chapter twenty-nine

We Are All Stars

I HAVE A HAT growing on my needles for a child that I don't know. A green hat with stars on it for Patrick, a little boy who calls himself "Pat Pat." I don't know Patrick, but I went to school with his grandpa, Mark.

A while back, Mark told me that Patrick was recovering from chemo and his daughter was collecting knitted hats, and did I know anyone who might want to make one to donate. I told Mark that I would get the word out. I thought about making one myself, someday, but things got busy and I didn't think about it again until I saw a mother holding the hand of a six-year-old child with no hair.

I contacted Mark's daughter, Betsy. We talked at great length, and I asked her where I could send a hat and how it came to be that she started PatPat's Hats. She told me that it started with a text message from her sister saying that she was bringing her nephew, Patrick, to the emergency room.

"Patrick had been extra cranky, what two-year-old isn't," Betsy said, "and was throwing up a little, but when he said that he had a 'boo boo on his head,' my sister called the doctor.

"Hurricane Irene was at our doorstep and the power was off at the doctor's office, so she couldn't see him. When my sister told the doctor that he was vomiting, she said that he probably just had a virus, but took him to the emergency room at the hospital in New Haven... just in case.

"When the scan was finished, doctors discovered he had three brain tumors. Not just one...three. 'Just like that,' my sister said, her whole world changed. Our whole family's world changed. The next day, surgeons removed the tumors and found that they were malignant.

"The rest of the family came to the hospital as soon as they could, Irene was whipping street signs and bending trees to the breaking point. My sister seemed calm and collected but I knew she was falling apart on the inside. I did the only thing I could do. I knit.

"All I could think of to do was to make Patrick a hat so his head wouldn't be cold when they shaved it. I cast on for a hat, and then I made another hat, and another hat. I couldn't stop. Most of those first hats were too small, so I thought about donating them to the hospital. After Patrick's treatments, I contacted Yale-New Haven; they said that they'd love to receive hats for babies and children. I had something to do. Something to give to other kids like my Pat Pat.

"My knitting friends called and asked what they could do, so I told them to knit hats. I thought maybe I might receive twenty or thirty, but my friends knit an unbelievable seventy-two hats. I started a Facebook page, 'PatPat's Hats,' and people from all over started contacting me and asking how they could help. 'Make hats!' I told them.

"After MRIs, surgery, chemo, radiation, and pathology

reports—and with our fears, tears, and prayers—Patrick got better every day. Years later, the tears still come sometimes. Tears of joy, tears for the families that we have met along the journey, tears remembering the fear throughout the year, and tears of thanks. Patrick is cancer free and thriving."

I ask Betsy who taught her to knit and she laughs.

"I learned from an actress backstage. I was on tour with a theater group, and in between scenes, she was always knitting. I asked her one day if she would teach me, it looked like she was having fun, and she said yes. Whenever we could, we spent our time backstage knitting together. She taught me everything. It was hard not to miss my queue.

"I went through a rough patch after that, I lost my grandmother, my parents got divorced, and my mom was diagnosed with breast cancer. I did what I knew how to do, I took care of her. I knew that she would need special blouses, so before her operation, I took her shopping. I was always thinking ahead, what would she need? Probably comes from taking care of my dolls. I took care of all my dolls. I knit while I took care of Mom, and we celebrated her last treatment.

"When cancer leaves your life there are so many things to celebrate. Clean scans, anniversaries of being cancer free, and anniversaries of diagnosis. For people going through treatment you celebrate such basic things—going back to school for half a day, being able to eat real food, and getting out of the hospital after a long stay. Our journey introduced us to many other people celebrating the strength and courage of those who have fought cancer, and those who have lost someone to cancer.

"The PatPat's Hats family will get to be part of another celebration for so many kids battling cancer. We're sending hats to Camp Rising Sun for the campers to wear during their time at camp. They have a simple motto, 'Where kids with cancer can have fun and smile.' Seems simple, right? But to these kids, spending one week where they are not the 'cancer kid' might just be their best week ever. So far, we've donated close to two thousand hats to kids in hospitals and camps and, with the help of the Internet, are expanding our reach far beyond our wildest dreams. Cancer affects everyone and we want to help in what little way we can."

Betsy said that her family started PatPat's Hats to celebrate Patrick—his strength, his courage, and his never-ending joy of everything that he loves in life, including sprinklers, Minnie Mouse, cupcakes, and music.

I hope you like the pattern at the end of the book and make a few hats...one for yourself and one for someone you don't know. It'll make you feel good. It's working for me!

I CAN'T BELIEVE HOW far I've come, how the making of things with my hands has transformed my life. No longer afraid, I move through my days with confidence and self-esteem. I've learned patience, not to give up, to keep trying no matter what.

In teaching me to knit, my aunt Barbara gave me the gift of myself, now strong and secure in the belief that I do belong, that I have value. I am grateful to her, and to so many others who helped me find my way. I wouldn't have made it without the yarn and the needles and the love they gave. From them, my strength has grown and now I can give back, healing others as I have been healed because it completes the circle, like knitting in the round.

Creating things with my hands has opened my heart to find the love and joy in everything. I've gained so much more than knitting skills; I've gained a world of friendships and a community where I feel like I belong. Row by row, stitch by stitch, we knit, we untangle, and we heal.

We Are All Stars!
Hat Pattern

This beanie pattern will fit everyone from preemie to adult! Directions here are for any size, any yarn, and any needles for any skill of knitter.

Materials
16-inch circular needles and a set of double points (or preferred needles for knitting in the round, or straights if you want to sew a seam)
Stitch marker
Tapestry needle
(Yardage is approximate and should make largest size.)
Bulky yarn, 110 yds using size 10 needles
Heavy worsted, 120 yds using size 9 needles
Worsted weight, 160 yds using size 7
DK weight, 175 yds using size 4 needles
Fingering weight, 200 yards using 2 needles
CO = Cast on

Sizes
Preemie = 14-inch circumference (This size needs double points throughout.)
Baby = 16" Child = 17" Child medium = 19"
Child large/Adult small = 21"
Adult medium = 22"
Adult large = 23"

Yarn	Bulky	Heavy Worsted	Worsted	DK	Fingering
Gauge	3.5 sts/ inch	4 sts/ inch	5 sts/ inch	6 sts/ inch	7 sts/ inch
Needles (U.S.)	10– 10.5	8–9	6–7	4–5	2–3
Sizes:					
Preemie	C/O 50 sts	C/O 56 sts	C/O 70 sts	C/O 84 sts	C/O 98 sts
Baby	C/O 56 sts	C/O 64 sts	C/O 80 sts	C/O 96 sts	C/O 112 sts
Child	C/O 60 sts	C/O 68 sts	C/O 84 sts	C/O 102 sts	C/O 120 sts
Child med.	C/O 66 sts	C/O 76 sts	C/O 96 sts	C/O 114 sts	C/O 132 sts
Adult sm.	C/O 74 sts	C/O 84 sts	C/O 104 sts	C/O 126 sts	C/O 146 sts
Adult med.	C/O 78 sts	C/O 88 sts	C/O 110 sts	C/O 132 sts	C/O 154 sts
Adult lg.	C/O 80 sts	C/O 92 sts	C/O 114 sts	C/O 138 sts	C/O 160 sts

Hat

Note: If you want to knit this flat, work back and forth in stockinette stitch instead of rounds, and sew a mattress stitch seam up the back when finished. This will allow you to incorporate stars as you knit, using the intarsia method, if you prefer. Stars cover 17 stitches wide by 19 rows tall.

Using the chart, find your size, yarn weight, and needle size.

Cast on proper number of stitches, place a marker and join into a round, being careful not to twist stitches.

If desired, work 1–2" in [k1, p1] rib, or simply begin knitting for a rolled brim.

Work until piece (from roll-up, or beginning of rib) measures:

Preemie = 3.5–4 inches.

Baby = 4–4.5 inches.

Child = 4.5–5 inches.

Child large= 5–5.5 inches.

Adult small = 6–6.5 inches.

Adult medium = 6.5–7 inches.

Adult large = 7–7.5 inches.

Crown Shaping

(If you didn't have a marker at the beginning of the round, put one on now.)

Round 1: *[K5, k2tog] repeat from * to end of round. (It's okay if the count doesn't come out even.)

Round 2: Knit (or purl if not working in the round).

Round 3: *[K4, k2tog] rep from * around.

Round 4: Knit (or purl if not working in the round).

Round 5: *[K3, k2tog] rep from * around.

Round 6: Knit. (You might have to insert double points here, don't be afraid, just knit some sts on each of 3 needles, then knit with the 4th.)

Round 7: *[K2, k2tog] rep from * around.

Round 8: Knit (or purl if not working in the round).

Round 9: *[K1, k2tog] rep from * around.

Round 10: Knit (or purl if not working in the round).

Round 11: K2tog, k2tog, k2tog, etc. for a few rounds

until you have 4 (for bulky yarn) to 8 (for fingering weight) stitches remaining. If you want a little top-knot, continue working around on these few sts until desired length. Cut yarn, leaving a long enough tail to weave in, thread tapestry needle and pull yarn through stitches. Go around again and cinch tight. Take yarn to inside of hat and weave in. (If hat is knit flat, use a mattress stitch to sew up the back seam from the right side.) Weave in any loose ends, steam lightly or block according to directions on ball band. Great job!

Using Star chart, duplicate stitch (sometimes called Swiss darning) stars at random where desired.

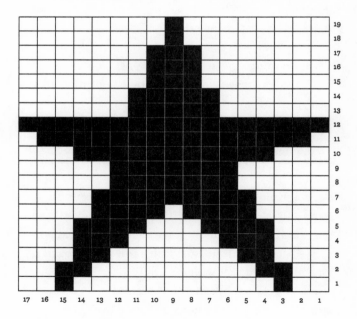

Happy knitting!

For pattern support, contact leegant101@yahoo.com

If you'd like to help PatPat's Hats, contact patpats.hats@gmail.com, or join their Facebook page at www.facebook.com/patpatshats, or simply mail a hat (or more) to:

PatPat's Hats
P. O. Box 318
Westbrook, CT 06498

They take all sizes and types—homemade or store-bought, preemie to teenagers—and ask that they be washable and soft (the softer, the better). All styles are welcome, including baseball caps with a cloth strap in the back, and they thank you.

A RENOWNED DESIGNER AND sought-after teacher, Lee Gant is a household name among knitting enthusiasts. Holding the rank of "master knitter," Lee enjoys working with adults and children, teaching self-empowerment through knitting. Some of Lee's designs can be found in *60 Quick Baby Knits*, in Knit Picks and Patternfish online, and at Strings and Things in Kauai. Lee's knitting has won many first place and best-in-show awards at county fairs in northern California, where she resides with her husband and their canine companion yellow lab, Zena IV. Her new pattern collection for children's knitwear will publish in the spring of 2016.

Photograph by Jonathan Kirker Photography, jonathankirker.com.

TO OUR READERS

Viva Editions publishes books that inform, enlighten, and entertain. We do our best to bring you, the reader, quality books that celebrate life, inspire the mind, revive the spirit, and enhance lives all around. Our authors are practical visionaries: people who offer deep wisdom in a hopeful and helpful manner. Viva was launched with an attitude of growth and we want to spread our joy and offer our support and advice where we can to help you live the Viva way: vivaciously!

We're grateful for all our readers and want to keep bringing you books for inspired living. We invite you to write to us with your comments and suggestions, and what you'd like to see more of. You can also sign up for our online newsletter to learn about new titles, author events, and special offers.

Viva Editions
2246 Sixth St.
Berkeley, CA 94710
www.vivaeditions.com
(800) 780-2279
Follow us on Twitter @vivaeditions
Friend/fan us on Facebook